# The KITCHY KITCHEN

# The KITCHY KITCHEN

## New Classics for Living Deliciously

## CLAIRE THOMAS

**EMILY BESTLER BOOKS**

—

**ATRIA**

NEW YORK  LONDON  TORONTO  SYDNEY  NEW DELHI

**ATRIA** BOOKS

A Division of Simon & Schuster, Inc.
1230 Avenue of the Americas
New York, NY 10020

First Emily Bestler Books/Atria Books hardcover edition August 2014

**EMILY BESTLER BOOKS / ATRIA** BOOKS and colophons are trademarks of Simon & Schuster, Inc.

For information about special discounts for bulk purchases, please contact Simon & Schuster Special Sales at 1-866-506-1949 or business@simonandschuster.com.

The Simon & Schuster Speakers Bureau can bring authors to your live event. For more information or to book an event contact the Simon & Schuster Speakers Bureau at 1-866-248-3049 or visit our website at www.simonspeakers.com.

Interior design by Elizabeth Van Itallie

Manufactured in China

10 9 8 7 6 5 4 3 2 1

Library of Congress Cataloging-in-Publication Data
Thomas, Claire.
  The kitchy kitchen / Claire Thomas.
      pages cm
  Includes index.
  1. Cooking. I. Title.
  TX714.T4937 2014
  641.5—dc23
                        2014000561

ISBN 978-1-4767-1073-0
ISBN 978-1-4767-1075-4 (ebook)

TO MY FAMILY

# CONTENTS

# A NOTE FROM CLAIRE

Have you cried yet? You know those tears. Kitchen tears. The ones that go down your cheeks and drop into the smoldering pile of whatever it was you were planning on serving. Maybe it's your tenth attempt at a recipe that still just doesn't want to work. Maybe it's your third date with someone you really wanted to impress and your entrée completely fell apart. Maybe it's just one of those days that you *needed* a warm cookie, but your fraught relationship with your oven prevented it.

I have cried over many a failed dish. It's nothing to be embarrassed about (okay, maybe a little . . . ), because that's what happens when we're frustrated, confused, and feel like something should be simple . . . and then it isn't and no one was there to help you.

When you flip through a food magazine or check out a cooking show, everyone looks so calm, don't they? People are smiling, there is no burnt toast, no wine spilled on the couch . . . there aren't any sliced fingers or "Oh crap, I forgot to add the salt" moments. This has not been my particular experience in learning to cook, and I imagine it isn't yours, either. After all, we're only human. We novices don't know all the secrets to making a recipe work or hosting a fabulous party . . . yet. Especially when you're just learning how to cook for yourself and your friends, it's easy to be discouraged if the finished product doesn't mirror (or even remotely resemble) the manicured photographs or carefully edited clips. So: How are we beginner cooks supposed to cope?

What no one ever told me, not even my experienced cook of a mom, is that all dishes derive from one very basic set of techniques. Once you've got a dish down, those techniques allow you to play around with and tweak the recipe in a lot of delicious ways.

Which is where cookbooks come in. Cookbooks can be super helpful, but they can make a lot of assumptions about what kind of cook you are and what you know, along with what your budget is and how much time you have. Usually they assume you have endless quantities of all of the above. I'm not a professionally trained chef, so all I know is what I've experienced in my own kitchen.

And those experiences have informed this cookbook. Though it may seem obvious, since I wrote it, this is my kind of cookbook. It's a useful one. You can tell what recipes are easy and which ones are for lazy Sunday afternoons. I'll show you how to take a simple dish and gussy it up into a gourmet one that the ultimate fussy foodie would approve. I'll help you plan a party that will be fun not just for your guests, but for you, too. I'll show you what to buy when, and how to make a last-minute dinner when a hungry friend pops by. I'll try to do for you what I wish was done for me. ("Past Claire, this is Future Claire speaking. Stop freaking out over your tenth failed mac and cheese. Clean up the dishes, and I'll tell you how to make a béchamel that works. Don't worry, you'll get the hang of it, and it'll taste awesome.")

While I love eating seasonally, I tend to cook based on what event I'm making my dish for, or where my appetite happens to direct me. So, you'll find that the chapters are organized by type of dish, and alternatives are listed with each recipe so you can play around with seasonality.

In some chapters you'll find a sidebar where I delve a little further into a technique or ways to enjoy a dish a number of ways.

We all know how frustrating it is to get halfway through a recipe only to realize you're in over your head. To make navigating this cookbook a little easier, whether you're a total newbie or an old pro, I've organized the recipes into three different categories:

**YUM** These recipes are great for new cooks or people looking for something simple and quick.

**MMM** If this isn't your first time in the kitchen, these recipes are a little more complex and have multiple components or techniques.

**WOW** Showstopper! These are the more complicated recipes that require a little extra love and attention in the kitchen, and potentially need special equipment or have multiple components.

It should be mentioned that none of the recipes in this cookbook is ultrachallenging (that's not my style), but ones labeled "wow" require the most time and effort.

Ultimately, my hope is that this book will make your daily life a little easier, a little more fabulous, and positively delicious. I think we are going to have a lot of fun cooking together through this book, but always remember, no matter how ugly it gets, no matter how many dishes scorch or soufflés flop, you can always order Thai food. Nothing sops up kitchen tears like a container of noodles.

Happy cooking, and more important, happy eating!

XOXO
Claire

# FIRST THINGS FIRST

Organizing Your Pantry
and Commanding Your Kitchen

Whether it's being prepared for a rainy weekend in or for the zombie apocalypse, everyone should always have a pantry stocked with enough basics to last them a couple of days. The trick is to fill it with stuff you actually use and love. These are the best ingredients, tools, and what-have-yous to keep your kitchen running even when there's nothing in the fridge.

# THE PERFECT PANTRY

For some, the pantry is where you keep all those things that gather dust way beyond their expiration dates. But with my selection, you'll use these up again and again. I've broken it down into the same three levels (Yum, Mmm, and Wow) that will take your cupboards from meh to amazing.

**YUM**

These are the essentials, the must-haves for quick weekday dinners and quick fixes to add flavor.

- Extra virgin olive oil (Look for oil in a dark glass bottle or in a can, as light and heat can ruin the flavor, and make note of the "use by" date (no more than 6 months), since olive oil does not improve with age. I keep a more expensive small-batch oil on the counter for drizzling on soups and using in vinaigrettes. For cooking, I use a cheaper olive oil I don't mind blowing through.)
- Kosher salt
- Black peppercorns (for freshly ground pepper)
- Dried pasta
- Good all-purpose unbleached flour (I like King Arthur or Bob's Red Mill best.)
- Baking powder and baking soda
- White and brown sugars
- Garlic
- Yellow onions
- Short-grain white rice (I like Cal Rose best.)
- Good broth, chicken and/or vegetable (Always go for low-sodium, and from free-range, organic chickens for the best flavor. "Free-range" means the chickens can roam freely for food, rather than living in confined enclosures. Letting them roam free and eat organic feed—which can't contain animal by-products, antibiotics, or genetically engineered grains and cannot be grown using persistent pesticides or chemical fertilizers—leads to more flavorful chicken.)

**MMM**

These extras are great additions to a fully stocked pantry on top of the ones above.

- Vanilla ice cream (Just 'cause.)
- Sriracha sauce (for extra heat)
- Dried beans (decidedly unsexy sounding, but delicious with toast)
- Quinoa (Perfect for last-minute sides or as a way to extend vegetables. Plus, protein!)
- Whole-grain mustard (I could bathe in this stuff. Slightly spicy but with a lovely round flavor, it's wonderful in sauces, vinaigrettes, and as seasoning.)
- Good dark chocolate (for nibbling, baking, and adding to your favorite desserts)
- Pure vanilla extract
- Canned whole tomatoes (for a quick pasta sauce; San Marzano tomatoes are my favorite)
- Whole spices (They last longer and have a stronger flavor.)
- Honey
- Soy sauce
- Thai fish sauce (for a delicious savory/umami flavor)

**WOW**

Some of these might be a little indulgent or used less often, but they can truly elevate a dish to "wow."

- Truffle oil or salt (Yep, indulgent. But a drop or pinch goes a long way and a good one will last you for months.)
- Balsamic vinegar di Modena (for drizzling at the very end on soups and salads)
- Anchovies packed in olive oil (for adding depth to sauces, soups, and broths)
- Good wine (I like to have a tasty syrah or sangiovese on hand for sipping and cooking.)
- Great beer (I love adding beer to recipes for an unexpected kick. Maltier options like amber ales or Belgian beers have a lovely depth of flavor that is great in cooking.)
- Unsweetened cocoa powder (It's really important to get the good stuff here, like Valrhona—it has a much richer and deeper flavor.)
- Panko breadcrumbs (great texture and perfect when you can't bother to make fresh crumbs)
- Boxed brownie mix (Let's be real; this needs to be in everyone's pantry.)

# THE HOUSEWARMING LIST

These utensils and appliances will help you to achieve kitchen greatness.

**YUM** THE ESSENTIALS

- A good chef's knife
- A good paring knife
- A good bread knife
- At least two cutting boards, wood or plastic
- Wooden spoons
- Two whisks
- Rubber spatulas
- A metal spatula
- Cheese grater
- Microplane
- Measuring cups and spoons
- Instant-read thermometer
- Deep-frying or candy thermometer
- Rimmed baking sheets
- A 9 by 13-inch baking dish
- Mixing bowls
- A fine-mesh strainer
- A large saucepan
- A large pot
- A Dutch oven
- Rolling pin
- Dish towels
- A pepper mill

## THE ADDITIONS

- A food processor
- Stand mixer with whisk, paddle, and dough hook attachment
- A hand mixer
- A blender
- Mortar and pestle
- A kitchen scale (for getting exact weight measurements)
- Spice grinder (the same as a pepper grinder, but used just for spices so you don't mix flavors)
- Cast-iron skillet
- Pizza stone
- Silicone mats for baking
- Mandoline (I use one I bought at my local grocery store.)
- Ricer or food mill

## THE SPECIALTY ITEMS

- Charcoal or gas grill
- Immersion blender (This makes blending so easy.)
- Fancy wine opener (for quick cork removal)
- Waffle iron
- Ice cream maker
- Meat grinder (You can get this as an attachment to your stand mixer.)
- Pasta roller and cutter
- Tabletop items: pretty linens, cheese boards, vintage plates and cutlery

# KITCHEN CHEAT SHEET

Whether you're reading my book or printing out recipes online, you'll come across a lot of language that can seem vague, especially when presented with myriad choices when you're in the market. Following or not following these tips won't necessarily mean the success or failure of a recipe, but they can only help.

Kitchen tips that ring true in this book unless noted otherwise:

- Always read the recipe twice through before getting started.
- Preheat your oven fully. This will ensure accurate cook times and even cooking.
- For meat or fish, I like to have separate cutting boards that are easy to clean, to prevent cross-contamination.
- After working with raw meat or fish, wash your hands with soap and hot water, and do the same with any utensil or surface they came in contact with.
- Buy spices whole and grind them with a grinder or mortar and pestle or spice grinder when you need them. The flavors are stronger and last way longer.
- Olive oil should always be extra virgin, which means it comes from the first press.
- Never store tomatoes or any other sturdy fruit in the fridge. It diminishes their texture and flavor, and they look so pretty on the counter.
- Strawberries *hate* water, so if you need to rinse them, do it just before using them.
- Leeks grow in sand, so you need to thoroughly clean them. The easiest way is to cut off the dark green tops, then split the leek all the way down, but stopping just before the

base. This way it holds together when you rinse it, but you can get into all of the layers.

- The easiest way to chop broccoli and cauliflower is to cut the head in half from the top to the base, and then halve it again from top to base. You'll have four wedges. Next, just slice the core out of each wedge, and break apart the florets with your hands.

- Taste and season your dishes as you cook. This means less correction at the end of a recipe, and lets you gauge how the flavors are developing and changing as you cook.

- With a stand mixer you have three attachments: paddle, whisk, and dough hook. The paddle is for mixing things together (cookie dough, batter, etc.); the whisk is for whipping air into things (cream, egg whites); and the dough hook is for kneading yeast breads (cinnamon rolls, pizza).

- Butter should always be unsalted so you can control how seasoned your dish is.

- Eggs should always be large and at room temperature so that you have a consistent amount of liquid and their whites are viscous and more elastic.

- Crack an egg on a flat surface, not on an edge. Cracking on an edge forces the shell into the egg, which can end up in your food or, worse, cutting the yolk.

- To separate eggs, gently crack an egg on a flat surface and let the white fall into a bowl. Using the shells, transfer the yolk back and forth as the white continues to fall into the bowl. When all the white is gone and only the yolk remains, place the yolk in a separate bowl. You can also crack the egg into your clean hands and let the white fall through your fingers while you gently hold on to the yolk.

- Whipped egg whites should come from the freshest eggs, when the proteins in the whites are their strongest and most elastic.

- Eggs for hard-boiling should be a few days old, for easier peeling.

- In this book, *sugar* means white granulated sugar and *superfine sugar* is just finer white sugar, sometimes labeled "baking sugar." (You can make your own by pulsing it in a food processor.)

- In this book, brown sugar is always packed. You should compact it enough that the sugar holds the shape of the measuring vessel when you flip it upside down.

- *Creaming* the butter and sugar is a step that pops up in many baking recipes. This means you beat together room temperature butter and sugar with the paddle attachment of an electric mixer until the butter and sugar form a uniform mixture that is light and fluffy. This creates a base for the rest of the ingredients to cling to. And by beating the butter and sugar together, you aerate the mixture (meaning, mix air into it) and the finished product will have a lighter texture when baked. It's one of those little things that can make a difference in a recipe.

- Flour is never compacted. To properly measure, sift or lightly whisk the flour first, then scoop the measure into the flour. Level off with a finger or butter knife. Don't shake the measuring cup or hit it on the counter; it'll make the flour compact, which leads to denser baking.

- Milk and cream should always be refrigerator cold, especially for whipping.

- To *scrape* a vanilla bean, slice it down the center, from tip to tip, with a knife. Open the bean up and scrape the knife along the cut surface, collecting the seeds on the blade. Add the seeds to whatever you want to flavor. The pod can be stored in sugar to create vanilla sugar, or added to liquids that you'd like to flavor.

- To *zest*: This is when you use a Microplane or very fine grater to scrape off just the very outer skin of a citrus fruit. Doing this, you'll get a ton of flavor but none of the bitterness from the white pith.

- When a recipe says to *plate* something, this means put it on the serving plate in an appealing manner.

- To *reduce* a liquid, just continue cooking it until more of the water in the liquid evaporates and the remaining liquid is thicker, like a sauce. This concentrates the flavor of the liquid and makes the texture thicker and richer.

- When a recipe calls for egg whites or cream to be whipped to *soft peaks*, it means that they're whipped until they can mostly hold their own shape, but when the whisk is removed, the peak folds over on itself. This kind of peak has a looser, less structured texture. A *stiff peak* is when the egg white or cream is whipped until the peaks can hold themselves up completely. When the whisk is removed, the peak stands upright. Careful about overbeating, though! If you go past the stiff peak phase, you'll get dry meringue and clumpy whipped cream.

- *Folding* is a gentle way of incorporating one ingredient into another. This is typically done with delicate items like cake batter containing whipped egg whites. To fold, take a large rubber spatula and run it along the bottom of the bowl, lifting as much of the mixture as possible, and bringing it up and over. Continue doing this to just blend the ingredients together.

- To *macerate* and to *marinate*: Both of these actions look the same: submerging an ingredient in liquid. But macerating is when you're trying to soften an ingredient, and marinating is when you soak an ingredient to add flavor to it. I typically macerate fruit to make it soft and juicy, and marinate meat to add flavor before cooking it.

- To *blanch* something is to cook it quickly in boiling water, then *shock* it in an ice bath (a bowl of cold water and ice) to immediately stop the cooking process. I'll do this to vegetables to make their colors become vivid and to make them tender but still crisp. Blanching also brings out their sweetness. It makes a big difference, especially if you're planning on serving the vegetables unadorned.

- Waxy versus starchy potatoes: Believe it or not, a potato is not just a potato. There's a ton of varieties, and which potato you pick makes a big difference, depending on your goal for a dish. Almost all potatoes can be categorized as waxy or starchy. Waxy potatoes, such as rose potatoes or fingerlings, are best for roasting or adding to soups and salads because they hold their shape. But they're also great pureed and smashed into gnocchi or mashed potatoes because of their creamy texture. Starchy potatoes, such as russets, have a fluffy texture that makes them ideal for french fries or baked potatoes. So pick your potato wisely!

- Order from the butcher. Whenever a recipe calls for butchering—cutting a chicken into eight pieces (typically the breast halves, thighs, legs, and wings), or cubing 2 pounds of meat into 1-inch pieces, or grinding beef into burger meat—I always have my butcher do it in front of me. It saves me time and money; buying a whole piece of meat and having it

broken down is usually much cheaper than buying piece by piece—and it's one less thing I have to deal with when I get home.

- If you can't find shallots or leeks, yellow onions are an okay replacement. If you can't find chives, you can use green onions.

- Use a chef's knife (8- or 10-inch) for all chopping and slicing, and use a paring knife for detail work.

- A sharp knife is a safe knife. Always keep your fingers out of the line of the blade and work with precision.

## A QUICK GUIDE TO KITCHEN MEASUREMENTS

It's easy to get mixed up with kitchen measurements. Teaspoons, tablespoons, fluid ounces, and cups measure volume (how much space an ingredient takes up), while ounces and pounds measure weight. This list helped me so much, especially when halving or doubling a recipe. Hope you brushed up on your fourth-grade math!

3 teaspoons = 1 tablespoon
½ fluid ounce = 1 tablespoon
4 tablespoons = ¼ cup
2 fluid ounces = ¼ cup
8 fluid ounces = 1 cup
2 cups = 1 pint
16 ounces = 1 pound
4 cups = 1 quart
4 quarts = 1 gallon

## HOW TO SHOP AT THE FARMERS' MARKET

Farmers' markets can be intimidating, especially for first-time shoppers. Here are some of my tips for getting everything on your list easily.

- Come prepared: This means you've already been to the ATM, you have at least two reusable bags, and you have a list.

- You want to come early, especially for popular markets, because the rare or limited items go fast. If you missed out, ask vendors if they can hold some of the items for you next week, so you don't have to worry about availability.

- Do a pass around the market first. Don't buy the first thing you see because it's at the top of your list. Walk around, tasting as you go, and pick the best produce after you've seen what's available.

- Always ask if you can have a sample—don't assume!

- Make sure you buy your heavy or hearty items first and delicate ones last. You don't want to crush your cherry tomatoes with a watermelon!

- When you've bought your items, ask the farmer how best to cook it. It's the easiest way to enjoy simple, delicious food, and you're getting it right from the source.

# HOW TO CHOP

Using a knife can be one of the most intimidating aspects of working in a kitchen. Burns and bruises are the worst, but a cut? Ouch! To help get rid of some of the chopping block jitters, I thought I'd explain how to chop and slice ingredients in the simplest way. It can differ from vegetable to vegetable, but to illustrate the steps best, I'll use an onion as an example.

*Dice (top row, opposite)*: With a chef's knife, slice the onion in half lengthwise (meaning through the tip to the base) and chop off the tip of the onion. Keeping the base intact, peel the skin off the onion. Make slices ¼-inch apart toward the base of the onion, all the way down. Then, with the knife tip pointed toward the root, slice the onion to the base, but not through it. Finally, make ¼-inch parallel cuts across the onion. The perfectly diced onion will pop right off the knife.

*Slice (rows 2 and 3, opposite)*: Slice the onion in half lengthwise (meaning through the tip to the base) and chop off the tip and base of the onion. Peel the skin off the onion. Slice very thinly across the curved part of the onion (not the open slice where the base and tip used to be). You'll get consistent slices.

Here are some other techniques that pop up, especially with fresh herbs.

*Chiffonade (bottom row, opposite)*: This sounds complicated, but it's actually my favorite way to chop leafy herbs like basil. Simply take the leaves and stack them on top of one another like a deck of cards, all facing the same direction. Roll up the herbs so they look like a little cigar. Slice across the roll so you get thin ribbons.

*Rough chop*: I pack the herbs into a tight handful and chop across the pile twice.

*Fine chop*: The same as a rough chop, but keep going until the pieces are ¹⁄₁₆-inch wide.

1 Dicing

2

3

4

1 Slicing

2

3

4

5

6

7

8

1 Chiffonade

2

3

4

# KITCHEN COMBINATIONS

If you find yourself leaving the farmers' market with twice as much as you intended to buy, don't worry; that's my life every week. I came up with a list of classic combinations as jumping-off points for inspiration. When you just don't know what to do with everything cluttering your fridge and counter, take a look at the chart below and get creative!

| | | | |
|---|---|---|---|
| tomato + mozzarella + basil = salad, sandwich, pasta, pizza | browned butter + sage + squash/ pumpkin/yams = side, salad, soup, pizza | carrot + ginger + cumin = salad, soup, side | citrus + fennel + arugula = salad, sandwich, garnish |
| balsamic vinegar + strawberries + black pepper = dessert, salad, sauce, baking | beets + creamy cheese + balsamic = salad, side | sea salt + chocolate = dessert, ice cream, sauce, baking | onion + corn + cilantro = salad, side, pizza, soup, eggs |
| cilantro + avocado + lime = salad, garnish, salsa | tomatoes + cucumbers + fresh herbs = salad, soup, side | spinach + pine nuts + Parmigiano = salad, side, soup, pasta, eggs | pecans + squash/ pumpkin/ yams + maple syrup = side, dessert, baking |
| blue cheese + fall fruit = side, salad, sandwich, pizza | walnuts + honey + cheese = dessert, baking, pizza, side, salad, sandwich | honey + apples + cheddar = dessert, baking, sandwich, side | mushrooms + goat cheese + thyme = salad, side, baking, pizza, pasta, eggs |
| sweet peas + bacon + cream = side, pasta, eggs, soup | chicken + lemon + garlic = main, pasta, pizza, salad, sandwich | garlic + chile + tomato + lemon = soup, salad, pizza, side, eggs | seafood + fennel + tomato = soup, main, pizza |

# WAKE-UP CALL

## The Perfect Breakfast for Any Situation

Is breakfast the most *important* meal of the day? I don't really care. But I will say it's my *favorite* meal of the day, even if it's at 10:00 p.m. Breakfast is the perfect combination of all the things I love: bacon + anything else . . . usually a carbohydrate. There aren't really any rules; toast with jam and a cup of black coffee or a savory tart and a glass of Champagne are both fair game, especially if we're talking about that even better time of the weekend: brunch. The possibilities are endless, whether you're looking for something light and fresh or utterly indulgent. In this chapter, I cover both ends of the spectrum, and some of the delicious stuff in between.

# BUTTERMILK PANCAKES TRANSFORMED INTO BLUEBERRY, CHOCOLATE CHIP, HONEY BANANA WALNUT

AN ⬤ MMM RECIPE

Here are my three favorite iterations of pancakes, all ready to go on the fly. The blueberry compote brings the blueberry flavor up a few notches, the chocolate paired with cinnamon brings a Mexican hot chocolate vibe, and the walnuts with banana slices are great, but the drizzle of honey that caramelizes on the griddle puts them over the top.

## BASIC PANCAKES

*For 16 medium pancakes*

### DRY INGREDIENTS
2 cups all-purpose flour
3½ teaspoons baking powder
¼ cup white sugar
2 tablespoons light brown sugar, packed
½ teaspoon kosher salt

### WET INGREDIENTS
3 large eggs, whites and yolks separated
1¼ cups buttermilk
¼ cup sour cream
6 tablespoons (¾ stick) unsalted butter, melted, plus more butter for cooking and serving
1 teaspoon pure vanilla extract

Maple syrup, for serving

1. Sift the dry ingredients into a bowl.

2. In another large bowl, mix together the wet ingredients, reserving the egg whites. In a third bowl, beat the egg whites with a whisk or hand mixer to soft peaks (careful not to overbeat them!). With a rubber spatula, combine the wet and dry ingredients until just mixed (no dry ingredients are showing) and then fold in the egg whites.

3. Heat a griddle or large sauté pan over medium heat. Add a tablespoon of butter to the pan, and once the butter is melted, ladle in the batter. Each pancake should be about 6 inches across. Drizzle the mix-ins (see page 18) on top of the pancakes while they're cooking. Cook until bubbly on top (2 to 3 minutes) and golden brown on the bottom, then flip. Cook for another 2 to 3 minutes.

4. To serve, place a pancake on a plate and sprinkle with leftover mix-ins. Add another pancake and continue to layer with mix-ins. This will help the flavors be absorbed into the pancakes. Serve with warm maple syrup and a slab of butter.

*(continued on page 18)*

## blueberry compote

*For 2 cups compote*

4 half-pints blueberries
Juice of 3 limes
1 cup white sugar

**1.** Combine everything in a bowl to coat.

**2.** Pour into a medium pot, and heat over medium heat for about 10 minutes. Basically, the berries should look juicy and there should be a thin syrup.

**3.** Cool to room temperature. If using later, put into a clean, sealed container in your fridge. Good for up to 2 weeks.

## chocolate chip pancakes

1 cup roughly chopped semisweet
  chocolate
½ teaspoon ground cinnamon
Pinch of cayenne pepper (optional)

Combine the chocolate and cinnamon. Sprinkle on the pancakes as much or as little as you like. If you like heat, add a pinch of cayenne.

## honey banana walnut pancakes

3 ripe bananas, sliced
1 cup walnuts
¼ cup honey

Add onto the pancakes as much or as little as you like after you ladle the batter. The honey caramelizes the banana nicely, so add that last, before you flip the pancakes.

## BLACKBERRY JAM AND CREAM CHEESE–STUFFED PAIN PERDU

A **YUM** RECIPE

Pain perdu is a very basic version of French toast but with one difference: You soak the bread in a milk mixture first and then dunk it in egg, rather than mixing the milk and egg together and just dunking the bread in that. This sounds like a totally unimportant detail because it is such a subtle change, but by dunking it in the egg separately, you get this crunchy, golden-brown crust and an almost savory quality to the bread. It's a detail, but it's transformative.

*For 3 servings*

4 ounces cream cheese, softened
6 slices sourdough bread (1-inch thick)
½ cup blackberry jam (or any jam you like)
2 tablespoons light brown sugar, packed
½ teaspoon ground cinnamon
¼ teaspoon freshly grated nutmeg
½ teaspoon kosher salt
1 cup milk
1 cup half-and-half
1½ teaspoons pure vanilla extract
3 large eggs
Unsalted butter, for greasing the pan and
    serving
Maple syrup, for serving
Powdered sugar, for dusting

1. Spread 1 to 2 tablespoons of cream cheese on one slice and 1 to 2 tablespoons of jam on the other; sandwich the bread together. Make 3 sandwiches this way.

2. Mix 1 tablespoon of the brown sugar, the cinnamon, nutmeg, salt, milk, half-and-half, and vanilla together. Soak each sandwich on each side for about 5 seconds or until thoroughly soaked through. Whisk the eggs and remaining 1 tablespoon brown sugar together in a shallow bowl.

3. Heat a pan or griddle over medium heat and grease with butter. Take the soaked sandwich (drain it briefly by holding it up and letting it drip for a few seconds) and dunk in the egg mixture, coating both sides.

4. Cook in the pan until golden brown, flipping once (2 to 3 minutes per side). Serve with butter, syrup, and powdered sugar.

## BELGIAN SUGAR WAFFLES WITH MACERATED BERRIES

A (WOW) RECIPE

You'll notice these waffles aren't swimming in syrup, which, considering that a waffle seems strategically built for syrup holding (what are those divots for, anyway?), seems odd. But these are Liège-style waffles, named after the town in Belgium that made them famous, and unlike American waffles, they're sweet on their own.

*For 10 single waffles*

1½ teaspoons active dry yeast
1½ cups lukewarm milk
1 tablespoon honey
1½ tablespoons white sugar
½ teaspoon kosher salt
2 cups all-purpose flour
2 large eggs
4 ounces (1 stick) unsalted butter, softened, plus more for the bowl and waffle iron
1 cup Belgian pearl sugar or sugar cubes crushed into ¼-inch pieces
Macerated Fruit (recipe follows), for serving

1. Put in the yeast and milk into the bowl of a stand mixer with the dough hook attached, and combine until the yeast is just moistened. This should take only a few seconds.

2. Add the honey, sugar, salt, and flour and mix at medium speed to combine. While mixing, add the eggs and the butter (in pieces), until the mixture is smooth (this will take about 10 minutes).

3. Remove the bowl from the mixer and cover it with plastic wrap. Let it rest at room temperature for 1 hour, until the mixture begins to bubble.

4. Just before cooking, mix the pearl sugar into the dough until the chunks are well distributed.

5. Preheat an electric waffle iron (one made for Belgian-style waffles) to high heat. Lightly grease the iron and pour in the batter, filling it two-thirds full. Cook for 5 to 6 minutes, or until the sugar caramelizes (it'll be quite dark). Serve with the macerated fruit.

## macerated fruit

*For 4 cups fruit*

These are my favorites, but any fruit you like will do.

1 cup raspberries
1 cup blackberries
1 cup sliced pitted plums
1 cup sliced pitted white peaches
Juice of 2 oranges, or ½ cup sweet white wine, such as a riesling

Combine everything and let it rest for 1 hour in the fridge. Feel free to use your favorite fruit combination—sky's the limit!

## CARAMELIZED OATMEAL
## WITH SAUTÉED BANANAS

A **YUM** RECIPE

In this version of oatmeal, I melt a little butter and brown sugar together and sauté bananas with vanilla bean, then toast the oats in this delicious mixture before I add the water. It's like warm banana bread in a bowl—it's awesome. Try it with pears and pecans, or any of your other favorite toppings!

*For 2 servings*

2 tablespoons unsalted butter
3 tablespoons light brown sugar, packed,
 plus more for serving
1 vanilla bean, scraped, or 1 teaspoon pure
 vanilla extract
2 bananas, sliced ¼-inch thick (just ripe,
 but not at all mushy)
1½ cups oatmeal (not the quick-cooking
 kind)
¼ teaspoon kosher salt
Milk
Walnuts (optional)

1. In a medium pot over medium-low heat, melt the butter. Add the brown sugar and scraped vanilla, pods and all (if using vanilla extract, that'll be added later). Once it's all melted together, add the banana slices and sauté until soft and golden brown. Don't stir them; just let them caramelize a bit in the pan. Scoop out half the bananas and set aside.

2. Add the oatmeal to the remaining bananas and lightly stir until slightly toasted or fragrant, about 3 minutes. Add ½ cup water and stir until absorbed, then add another 2½ cups, along with the salt and the vanilla extract if not using a vanilla bean. Remove the vanilla pod. Cook until all the water is absorbed and the oatmeal is soft.

3. Top the oatmeal with a splash of milk and the reserved banana mixture. Garnish with brown sugar and walnuts if you like, and go to town!

## ROSEMARY-BACON HASH BROWNS

AN  RECIPE

These are not your typical hash browns. They are crusty, crunchy, and savory browns that look a little rough around the edges. But what they lack in style, they certainly make up for in flavor, especially with a touch of rosemary and some bacon.

*For 3 to 4 servings*

3 russet potatoes
4 slices thick-cut bacon, diced
½ yellow onion, sliced
1 garlic clove, minced
1 tablespoon finely chopped fresh
    rosemary
Kosher salt and freshly ground black pepper
¼ cup extra virgin olive oil, for drizzling
    between flips

**1.** Spear the potatoes with a fork a few times into the skin. Pop the potatoes into the microwave and cook for 10 minutes, or boil in water until the skin is pulling away and the potato is soft. Roughly chop the potatoes and discard any large sheets of skin.

**2.** Heat a large sauté pan over medium heat and cook the bacon for 7 to 10 minutes; it should be almost crisp. Add the onion and garlic (add a tablespoon of butter if using leaner bacon), and cook until the onion is soft, about 5 minutes. Add the potatoes and mix to combine, then press everything down, forming a sort of patty. Sprinkle with the rosemary and salt and pepper, then let the potatoes cook, untouched, for 5 minutes, until just starting to get golden brown on the bottom.

**3.** Drizzle with olive oil and turn the potatoes over in the pan. Pat down, salt and pepper that side, and cook for 5 minutes more, until that side is golden brown. Repeat this process until the potatoes are a deep golden brown and crunchy; the whole thing takes 30 to 35 minutes. With the back of your spatula, break the potatoes apart and stir around. Done!

## ROSEMARY, POTATO, AND KALE TART

A (WOW) RECIPE

I love making, serving, and eating savory tarts. Perfect as make-ahead dishes, they can be served room temp, and they taste delicious, too. Plus, you can put practically anything in them. Crispy and golden brown on top, hearty and filling inside, all nestled in a flakey, tender tart crust. Potato chips? Bah! Sign me up for a savory tart instead.

*For one 9-inch tart*

### SAVORY PIE DOUGH
1¼ cups all-purpose flour, plus more for rolling
1½ teaspoons white sugar
½ teaspoon kosher salt
4 ounces (1 stick) unsalted butter, cold
Up to ¼ cup ice water

### FILLING
2 tablespoons unsalted butter
½ yellow onion, chopped
2 garlic cloves, minced
6 ounces kale, stemmed and chopped
Extra virgin olive oil, for drizzling
Kosher salt and freshly ground black pepper
Pinch of chili flakes
1 cup ricotta cheese
3 sprigs rosemary, finely chopped leaves from 1 sprig, whole leaves from 2 sprigs
3 or 4 small rose potatoes, sliced paper thin (I used a mandoline.)
½ cup grated Parmigiano

1. For the pie crust, in a food processor or quickly using your fingertips, combine the flour, sugar, salt, and butter until the chunks of butter are the size of peas and the flour feels like wet sand. Add a few tablespoons of water and mix until the dough comes together easily. It's too dry if it immediately clumps apart. Add water 2 tablespoons at a time; you can always add more water but not more flour, so be careful not to add too much! Plop the dough on top of a sheet of plastic wrap. Loosely wrap the ball and press down, smooshing the ball into a disc about an inch thick. Pop it into the fridge for 30 minutes while you busy yourself with the other stuff.

2. Preheat the oven to 425°F.

3. Unwrap the dough and place it on a well-floured surface. Sprinkle with flour and roll out with a rolling pin (turning often to get an even thickness) until the dough is about ¼-inch thick and about 11 inches in diameter. Place the dough into a tart tin with a removable bottom and press in the bottom and sides. Trim off the top of the dough, place a small sheet of parchment paper on top of the bottom of the tart, and fill with pie weights or dried beans. (This will prevent the dough from rising and will keep the sides from shrinking down.)

4. Bake on the center rack for 10 minutes, then turn down the heat to 375°F, remove the parchment and weights, and bake for an additional 10 minutes.

5. Remove the tart from the oven and set on the counter. It doesn't have to be cool to continue.

6. Set the oven back to 425°F.

**7.** In a large sauté pan over medium heat, melt the butter and add the onion. Cook for 10 to 15 minutes. Add the garlic, cook for 1 minute, then add the kale and drizzle with a tablespoon of olive oil. Season with salt, pepper, and the chili flakes. Cook for 5 to 10 minutes, until the kale is wilted. Remove from the heat and mix in the ricotta and chopped rosemary.

**8.** Pour the mixture into the tart shell and top with a layer of potatoes. Drizzle with a couple of tablespoons of olive oil (you want the potatoes well coated, as this will make them crisp) and top with the whole rosemary leaves and the Parmigiano. Sprinkle a little salt and pepper on top.

**9.** Bake for 20 minutes, then broil for 1 minute or until golden brown and crispy on top. Enjoy warm, or cool to room temperature to serve.

## CHERRY TOMATO UPSIDE-DOWN TART

A 🟣 WOW RECIPE

Sometimes I get inspiration from the visualization of a recipe rather than the flavors. While writing this cookbook, I couldn't shake the image of a tarte tatin (a French upside-down apple tart) with tomatoes. The ultimate in brunch sophistication and the perfect centerpiece for a vegetarian meal, the roasted tomatoes, hearty sautéed spinach, and flakey, tender crust make this dish a dynamite combination.

*For one 9-inch tart*

1 to 2 pints cherry tomatoes (enough to cover the bottom of a 9-inch skillet in one layer, and about ½ pint more. The tomatoes will cook down quite a bit.)
Kosher salt and freshly ground black pepper
¼ cup extra virgin olive oil
4 ounces spinach or kale, roughly chopped (8 loosely packed cups)
½ cup lightly packed fresh basil chiffonade, plus whole leaves for garnish
2 garlic cloves, minced
Pinch of chili flakes
1 tablespoon balsamic vinegar
½ recipe Pie Crust (page 188), made with only 1 tablespoon sugar

**1.** Preheat the oven to 425°F. Place the cherry tomatoes on a baking sheet lined with parchment paper or a silicone mat and sprinkle with a pinch of salt, a pinch of pepper, and 2 tablespoons of the olive oil. Roast for 20 to 30 minutes, until the tomatoes are wrinkled and their bottoms are caramelized. Set aside to cool. Turn down the oven temperature to 400°F.

**2.** Meanwhile, in a large sauté pan over medium heat, add a tablespoon of the olive oil, then the spinach. Cook, stirring, for 3 minutes, or until slightly wilted. Add the basil, garlic, chili flakes, and a pinch of salt and pepper, and continue to cook for another 5 minutes, or until the spinach and basil are fully wilted. Set aside.

**3.** Arrange the roasted cherry tomatoes in one layer in a 9-inch cast-iron pan lightly coated with the remaining 1 tablespoon olive oil and the balsamic vinegar. (The pan should be about 2 inches deep.) Do not overlap the tomatoes. Sprinkle the basil-spinach mixture over the tomatoes.

**4.** On a well-floured surface, roll out your dough about ⅛-inch thick. Cut it into a circle just a bit bigger than the size of your pan. Place the dough over the tomatoes and gently tuck the edges around the side of the pan.

**5.** Bake for 30 to 40 minutes, until the crust is golden brown. Remove from the oven and cool to room temperature. Run a knife around the edge, then flip onto a serving plate. Garnish with basil.

## VANILLA SUGAR–ROASTED GRAPEFRUIT WITH ROSEMARY

A **YUM** RECIPE

Half a grapefruit always reminds me of the "reducing" (ahem, diet) menus I've come across time and again in my growing collection of vintage cookbooks. To me, grapefruit is delicious whether you're looking to reduce, increase, or just enjoy. In this recipe, the clean, slightly bitter flavor of grapefruit works perfectly with just a touch of burnt sugar. The rosemary adds an earthy, herbaceous note that sings with the vanilla and citrus.

*For 6 servings*

3 ruby red grapefruits
6 tablespoons vanilla sugar or white sugar
½ vanilla bean (if not using vanilla sugar)
Leaves from 2 sprigs fresh rosemary

**1.** Preheat the oven to 450°F. Halve the grapefruits and place them on a baking sheet cut side up.

**2.** If you don't have vanilla sugar on hand, make a quick batch by splitting the half vanilla bean lengthwise, scraping out the seeds, and mixing the scrapings with the sugar (this is easiest to do in a food processor so you don't get any clumps of vanilla). Store the leftover vanilla pod in a jar of sugar so you'll have vanilla sugar on hand next time. Sprinkle each grapefruit half with the sugar and top with rosemary leaves.

**3.** Roast for 10 minutes or until the grapefruit halves are puffed and browned on the edges. Serve immediately.

## CHEDDAR-CHIVE GRITS WITH POACHED EGGS

AN  RECIPE

Grits are as flavorless and watery or flavorful and creamy as you make them. Mildly sweet, slightly nutty grits made with savory chicken broth and garlic, sharp cheddar, biting chives, and tangy sour cream are the perfect base for a poached egg. When cooked properly, they're velvety and thick, never gummy, and in textural unison with the soft egg. Delicious, gooey, and savory, too.

*For 4 servings*

1¾ cups milk
2 cups chicken broth
1 garlic clove, minced
1 cup coarsely ground cornmeal (I used
   Bob's Red Mill Corn Grits/Polenta.)
4 ounces sharp cheddar, grated (about
   1 cup)
4 tablespoons (½ stick) unsalted butter
¼ cup sour cream
1½ teaspoons kosher salt
½ teaspoon freshly ground black pepper
1 tablespoon finely chopped chives
4 Poached Eggs (recipe follows)

1. In a medium saucepan, bring the milk and chicken broth to a boil. Add the garlic and slowly stir in the grits.

2. Reduce the heat to medium-low and cook, stirring frequently, until the grits are tender, about 15 minutes. You will have to babysit it. If they get gummy or set up, add a little milk and stir it in.

3. Remove the saucepan from the heat and stir in the cheese, butter, and sour cream. Season

with the salt and pepper and stir in the chives. Scoop into bowls, top with a poached egg, and serve immediately.

## poached eggs

1 egg per person

1. Bring a small pot of water to a soft boil (just past a simmer, so medium bubbles cling to the side of the pot). Crack an egg into a small bowl. For a perfectly shaped egg, toss the lid from a jar into the bottom of the pot of water, rim up. Stir the water with a spoon to create a whirlpool directly over the lid.

2. Gently pour the egg into the water. The lid will contain the egg as it cooks. Cook for 3 to 4 minutes for a perfect medium egg, up to 6 minutes for a hard one.

3. Remove the egg with a slotted spoon and place in a bowl.

4. To hold multiple poached eggs, cook each egg for only 2 minutes, then take it out of the water and place in a bowl of ice water. When you're ready to serve, place the eggs back in the boiling water for a minute or two to heat up.

## GRIDDLED CROISSANT WITH CHIVE CREAM CHEESE, SMOKED SALMON, AND PICKLED ONIONS

A YUM RECIPE

A griddled croissant is a beauteous thing. It's not a toasted croissant—it's better. Griddled means you sear the halves, with a little butter spread on them (of course) to get a perfectly crunchy, golden-brown, flakey, and buttery surface on which to build your sandwich. I topped my griddled croissant with fresh chive cream cheese, a little smoked salmon, and homemade pickled onions that take only minutes to make. The flavors are bright and rich, and it's such a unique way to enjoy a breakfast sandwich!

*Note:* This is a great use for day-old croissants, as searing them gives them a bit of life.

*For 2 servings*

2 croissants
1 tablespoon unsalted butter, softened
¼ cup cream cheese, softened
1 tablespoon snipped chives
4 pieces smoked salmon
¼ cup Pickled Onions (recipe follows)

1. Slice the croissants in half lengthwise and spread each side with butter. Heat a sauté pan over medium heat and add the croissants, butter side down. With a spatula, press the croissants down into the pan. Sear until brown and crisp, about a minute. Set the croissants aside on a plate.

2. Mix together the cream cheese and chives. Spread the cream cheese onto the bottom half of the croissants, top with salmon, and finish with some pickled onions. Pop the top half of the croissant on top and enjoy!

## pickled onions

¾ cup apple cider vinegar
2 tablespoons sugar
Pinch of kosher salt
1 bay leaf
2 whole cloves
1 chile de árbol
1 large red onion, sliced into thin rings

1. In a small, nonreactive saucepan, heat the vinegar, sugar, salt, bay leaf, cloves, and chile until boiling.

2. Add the onion slices and lower the heat, then simmer gently for 30 seconds. Remove from the heat and let cool completely.

3. Transfer the onions and the liquid to a clean jar. Refrigerate until ready to use. Store up to two weeks.

## DAD'S SOFT-BOILED EGGS AND DINER TOAST

A **YUM** RECIPE

My dad always made these eggs when I was little, along with bacon and toast "soldiers" cut into perfect strips. I'd dip the soldiers into the yolk and devour them, always with a heap of crushed black pepper. Diner toast and these eggs are everything breakfast is supposed to be: crunchy, buttery, and just slightly savory.

### soft-boiled eggs

*For 2 servings*

4 large eggs
Kosher salt and freshly ground black pepper

**1.** Fill a saucepan about halfway with water and bring it to a boil. Lower the heat so that the water reduces to a rapid simmer. Gently lower the eggs into the water one at a time. The eggs should be covered by liquid. Cook the eggs for 4 to 6 minutes: 4 minutes for a yolk that is still runny, up to 6 minutes for a yolk that is just set.

**2.** Drain the eggs and place each in an egg cup. Serve warm. Crack the top of the eggs off with a spoon or butter knife. Season with salt and pepper.

### diner toast

*For 2 servings*

Four 1-inch-thick slices sourdough bread
2 tablespoons unsalted butter, softened (or more)
1 slice thick-cut bacon, cut in half crosswise

**1.** Lightly butter the slices of bread. Cook the bacon on a griddle or in a sauté pan over medium heat. Save it to serve with your eggs. Drain off the fat.

**2.** Place the bread on the griddle and press down with a spatula to sear. Flip when golden brown (this usually takes a minute or two) and sear on this side as well.

**3.** Serve with more butter if you really want to go to town.

**4.** To eat, you can dunk the toast or bacon into the eggs, or spoon out the eggs onto the toast, whichever you prefer.

## MOM'S FRIED EGG SANDWICH

A (YUM) RECIPE

This sandwich is a little inappropriate. Like, this sandwich should have a chaperone if it goes out at night. Don't lend your car to it, and definitely don't have it house-sit for you. And definitely, definitely don't serve it to a crush unless you're ready to commit. Because after eating this sandwich, they will never leave you alone. It's gooey, melty, crunchy, and spicy, and with a bit of kick from the red onion and arugula, it literally hits every "awesome" sensor your palate can handle. Please don't abuse this power.

*For 1 sandwich*

2 slices thick-cut bacon
2 slices Swiss cheese
2 slices sourdough bread (½-inch thick)
1 large egg
2 slices tomato (¼-inch thick)
4 thin slices red onion
1 small handful arugula
1 tablespoon Aïoli (recipe follows)
Hot sauce (I like sriracha.)

**1.** Cook the bacon in a sauté pan over medium heat to desired crispness, set aside, and keep the grease in the pan.

**2.** Place the cheese on one slice of bread and top with the other slice, like you're making grilled cheese. Over medium heat, cook the sandwich in the bacon fat, pressing down with a spatula to sear the bread.

**3.** Meanwhile, fry the egg in another greased pan over medium heat to desired doneness.

**4.** When the sandwich is done on both sides, take it off the pan and open it up. Place the bacon slices on the bottom, followed by the fried egg, tomato slices, red onion, and arugula.

**5.** On the other slice of bread, spread the aïoli and drizzle with hot sauce. Pop the yolk, top with the other slice of bread, and go to town.

---

### aïoli

¼ cup mayonnaise
1 teaspoon whole-grain mustard
Pinch of lemon zest
1 garlic clove, minced
Kosher salt and freshly ground black pepper
1 tablespoon extra virgin olive oil

Mix all the ingredients together, and season to taste.

## HOW TO QUICHE: ASPARAGUS—WHITE CORN QUICHE

A WOW RECIPE

Bring a warm, custardy quiche to your next brunch and you're guaranteed to be everyone's hero. You can put anything into a quiche, it is that versatile. You can use a store-bought crust, or no crust at all. You can add leftovers, or seasonal ingredients bought just for the quiche. And you can *always* add bacon and/or cheese . . . that's never a bad idea.

Here, I went with white corn for sweetness, asparagus for that delicate grassiness, and leeks because I love them, but feel free to explore your favorite savory combinations.

*Note:* You can make a lighter version of this quiche with low-fat milk, 2 eggs, and 1 egg white.

*For one 9-inch quiche*

½ recipe Pie Crust (page 188), made with
    only 1 tablespoon sugar
½ cup chopped leeks, washed thoroughly
1 tablespoon unsalted butter
1 cup white corn kernels, plus juices (cut
    from 1 to 2 large ears)
½ cup cut asparagus, sliced thinly on the
    diagonal (about ½ bunch)
2 cups half-and-half
3 large eggs
Big pinch of kosher salt
Pinch of freshly ground black pepper
Pinch of freshly grated nutmeg

**1.** Preheat the oven to 425°F. Roll the dough out on a heavily floured surface into a ⅛-inch-thick circle large enough to fill a tart or pie tin that has a removable bottom. (I used a large fluted tart tin.) Lightly press the dough into the tin and trim the edges. Prick the dough with a fork all over, cover with parchment paper, and weight down the paper with pie weights or dried beans. (This is so the crust holds its shape.)

**2.** Pop into the oven for 10 minutes. Remove the parchment and weights and bake an additional 5 minutes or until lightly golden.

**3.** Set aside and let cool slightly.

**4.** Turn down the oven to 375°F. In a large sauté pan over medium-low heat, cook the leeks in the butter until tender, about 5 minutes. Add the corn and cook, stirring, for 5 minutes more. Add the asparagus and cook until bright green, 2 to 3 minutes.

**5.** In a bowl, whisk together the half-and-half, eggs, salt, pepper, and nutmeg. Add the vegetables and combine.

**6.** Pour the filling into the crust and bake for 30 to 35 minutes, until golden brown and the edges are cooked but the middle jiggles a bit like Jell-O. Remove the quiche from the oven and let it cool for 15 minutes before cutting.

# BAKED EGGS, THREE WAYS

A **YUM** RECIPE

If you're nervous about overcooking eggs, or just cooking in general, I've got a secret for you: baked eggs. They look super fancy, you can put anything in them, and even though they're a perfect breakfast, they totally work as an appetizer or light dinner as well. Best of all, they're super easy to make. So open up your fridge and see what leftovers you can use. It's baked eggs time!

## THE AMERICAN: CARAMELIZED ONIONS, BACON, ROSEMARY & A TOUCH OF CHEDDAR

*For 1 serving*

Unsalted butter, for greasing
2 slices thick-cut bacon, cooked and
 halved to fit into the ramekin
2 tablespoons Caramelized Onions (recipe
 follows)
¼ teaspoon finely chopped fresh rosemary
1 large egg
2 tablespoons heavy cream
Kosher salt and freshly ground black pepper
1 tablespoon grated cheddar
Grilled or toasted bread

1. Preheat the oven to 375°F.

2. In a buttered 6-ounce ramekin, lay the bacon. Sprinkle with the caramelized onions and rosemary, and crack the egg on top. Drizzle with the cream. Sprinkle with salt, pepper, and the cheddar.

3. Bake for 8 minutes in the lower third of the oven, until the white is set and the yolk is runny. Turn up the oven to broil and cook for 2 minutes to crisp the top.

4. Serve with grilled or toasted bread for dipping.

## caramelized onions

One large onion cooks down to about ½ cup. I like to make a bunch of caramelized onions and keep it in my fridge for whenever I need it throughout the week.

Unsalted butter (1 tablespoon per onion)
Onions, sliced
Kosher salt

In a large saucepan over medium-low heat, melt the butter. Add the onions, sprinkle with a little salt, and cook for 30 to 45 minutes (seriously) until a deep golden brown. Keep an eye on the onions as they cook, stirring every now and then, to make sure they don't burn.

## THE SPANIARD: GARLIC, PARSLEY, SMOKED PAPRIKA, AND SPANISH HAM

*For 1 serving*

Unsalted butter, for greasing
1 slice *jamón ibérico* or prosciutto
1 garlic clove, minced
1 large egg
2 tablespoons heavy cream
Kosher salt and freshly ground black pepper
¼ teaspoon pimentón (smoked paprika)
1 teaspoon chopped fresh flat-leaf parsley
Grilled or toasted bread

1. Preheat the oven to 375°F.

2. In a buttered 6-ounce ramekin, lay the slice of ham. Sprinkle with the garlic and crack the egg on top. Drizzle with the cream. Sprinkle with salt, pepper, and the paprika.

3. Bake for 8 minutes in the lower third of the oven, until the white is set and the yolk is runny. Turn up the oven to broil and cook for 2 minutes to crisp the top.

4. Sprinkle with the parsley. Serve with grilled or toasted bread for dipping.

## THE ITALIAN: TOMATO, THYME, PARMIGIANO, AND NUTMEG

*For 1 serving*

Unsalted butter, for greasing
1 canned or roasted tomato
¼ teaspoon fresh thyme, chopped
1 large egg
2 tablespoons heavy cream
Kosher salt and freshly ground black pepper
1 tablespoon grated Parmigiano
1 tablespoon Brown Butter (recipe follows)
Grilled or toasted bread

1. Preheat the oven to 375°F.

2. In a buttered 6-ounce ramekin, lay the tomato. Sprinkle with the thyme and crack the egg on top. Drizzle with the cream. Sprinkle with salt, pepper, and the Parmigiano.

3. Bake for 8 minutes in the lower third of the oven, until the white is set and the yolk is runny. Turn up the oven to broil and cook for 2 minutes to crisp the top.

4. Drizzle with the brown butter. Serve with grilled or toasted bread for dipping.

### brown butter

To make brown butter, simply melt butter in a pan over medium heat, then let it continue cooking until the milk solids (the white bits) turn golden brown and the melted butter starts to smell nutty. Remove from the heat immediately.

# THE BOTTOM OF THE BOWL

Comforting, Delicious Soups

Soup can be many things—comforting and cozy, exotic and bright, immensely complex, or rustic and simple. I always stock my fridge with various kinds to last me all week. Leftovers are just as good the second (and third) time around. Whether you have only a few minutes or a few hours, a delicious soup is in your future.

# WHITE CORN–CHIPOTLE SOUP

AN (MMM) RECIPE

Smoky and sweet, with a kick of heat, this corn soup is the perfect appetizer for a night you're cooking on the grill, or as a meal with some warm tortillas for dipping.

*For 2 quarts soup*
*1 quart = 2 to 3 servings*

½ cup heavy cream
Sprig of fresh rosemary
2 tablespoons cumin seeds
2 bay leaves
6 ears white corn
¼ cup extra virgin olive oil
1 cup finely chopped yellow onion
Kosher salt
4 garlic cloves, minced
3 teaspoons ground cumin
3 tablespoons adobo sauce from canned chipotle chiles
3 tablespoons unsalted butter
3 cups chicken broth
2 cups milk
Cotija cheese, for garnish (Feta and cheddar are great, too!)
Fresh cilantro, for garnish

1. In a small saucepan over low heat, bring the heavy cream, rosemary, cumin seeds, and bay leaves to a simmer. Remove from the heat and let sit for 20 minutes to infuse.

2. With a large knife, remove the corn kernels from the ears, then run the knife over the empty ears to gather the corn's juice. Set aside.

3. In a large sauté pan, heat the olive oil over medium heat and cook the onion with a pinch of salt until golden brown, 10 to 15 minutes. Add the garlic and ground cumin and cook, stirring frequently, for 5 minutes. Stir in the corn kernels and juice and the adobo sauce and continue cooking over medium heat for 5 minutes more.

4. Using your finest strainer, strain the infused herbal cream into the corn and chipotle mixture. Add the butter and stir. Add the broth and milk and simmer for 20 minutes (don't let it boil).

5. Using an immersion blender, or ladle the soup into a standing blender, puree half the soup. It should be thickened but still have texture. Add back to the rest of the soup. Taste and adjust seasoning.

6. Garnish with crumbled Cotija and cilantro leaves.

# BROWN BUTTER–BUTTERNUT SQUASH SOUP

A **WOW** RECIPE

This is the perfect dinner party soup. Comforting and a little decadent, it also looks beautiful in the bowl. The combination of sweet, tart, smoky, and brown-buttery is a definite crowd pleaser.

*For 4 quarts soup*
  *1 quart = 2 to 3 servings*

2 butternut squash, halved and seeded
2 medium kabocha squash or pumpkins, halved and seeded
Extra virgin olive oil, for drizzling
Freshly ground black pepper
4 slices thick-cut bacon, chopped
1 yellow onion, chopped
4 garlic cloves, minced
1 large celery stalk, chopped
1 large carrot, peeled and chopped
Kosher salt
3 quarts chicken broth
3 sprigs fresh flat-leaf parsley
Pinch of chili flakes
1 bay leaf
Brown sugar (optional)
4 tablespoons (½ stick) unsalted butter
Sour cream, for garnish

**1.** Preheat the oven to 425°F. In a roasting pan drizzle the butternut and kabocha squash with olive oil and sprinkle with pepper. Chuck them into the oven and roast for 45 to 60 minutes, until fork-tender. They don't need to be "mashed potato" soft, just soft enough for a fork to pierce them.

**2.** As they roast, get started on the broth. Over medium heat in a large pot, cook the bacon until not quite crisp, about 10 minutes. Add the onion and garlic, and cook until golden brown, about 15 minutes. Add the celery and carrot and cook for another 5 minutes. Season with a little salt and pepper. Add the chicken broth, parsley, chili flakes, and bay leaf, bring to a simmer, and let it cook for 10 minutes or so.

**3.** Once they're out of the oven and slightly cooled, scoop out the soft interior of the butternut and kabocha squash. Pluck out the bay leaf and parsley from the soup and add the squash. Let it all simmer together for about 10 minutes.

**4.** Puree the soup using an immersion blender or a standing blender. If using a standing blender, pour the soup back into the pot and taste for seasoning. Adjust the salt and pepper, and add the brown sugar if it needs some sweetness. If it's too thick, add a little water until it's the perfect consistency.

**5.** To brown the butter, place the unsalted butter (salted butter will burn) in a small saucepan over medium heat. Let it melt and bubble until it froths up a bit and the white milk solids have turned a nutty golden brown. Immediately add to the soup and stir.

**6.** To serve, ladle the soup into each bowl and top with a spoonful of sour cream.

# CAULIFLOWER-BRIE SOUP

A YUM RECIPE

This soup is just soooo luxurious. Like driving in a Bugatti with a scarf whipping in the wind luxurious, or skiing in Gstaad, or maybe it's as luxurious as you'd expect a soup with Brie in it to be. But it also manages to be so simple. It's exactly 10 ingred., done in 45 minutes, and if you pop a little truffle oil into this thing . . . whoa. It's a little out of control.

*For 3 quarts soup*

    *1 quart = 2 to 3 servings*

4 tablespoons (½ stick) unsalted butter
1½ cups chopped yellow onion
Kosher salt and freshly ground black pepper
4 garlic cloves, minced
1 teaspoon roughly chopped fresh thyme
    leaves
3 tablespoons all-purpose flour
1½ quarts chicken broth
8 cups chopped cauliflower
2 cups milk
1¼ cups Brie (rind removed)

**1.** In a medium sauté pan, melt 1 tablespoon of the butter over medium heat. Add the onion and cook, stirring, for 10 minutes, or until translucent. Season with salt and pepper, add the garlic and thyme, and continue cooking for another 5 minutes, until fragrant.

**2.** In a large pot over medium-low heat, melt the remaining 3 tablespoons butter, and add the flour. With a whisk, stir the butter and flour together until a loose paste forms. Continue stirring for a minute until the paste is pale golden brown and smells a bit nutty.

**3.** Whisk in the chicken broth about a cup at a time. Add the cooked onion and the cauliflower and cook, covered, for 20 minutes, until the cauliflower is cooked through and tender.

**4.** Add the milk and Brie, stirring until the cheese is melted. Puree in batches in a blender, or use an immersion blender in the pot. Reheat gently if necessary.

## SPICY WATERMELON SOUP

A **YUM** RECIPE

Watermelon usually conjures up ideas of summertime sweetness, either crunchy and fresh or pureed into a juicy *agua fresca*. But watermelon is also fantastic in a savory context. With a little spice, and a sweet and sour balance between the lime and honey, this soup is a refreshing start to any barbecue.

*For 1 quart soup*
*1 quart = 2 to 3 servings*

5 cups chopped watermelon
¼ cup lime juice
1 teaspoon sriracha sauce, plus more for garnish
1 tablespoon fresh mint leaves
1 tablespoon fresh cilantro leaves, plus more for garnish
1 tablespoon honey
½ cup dry riesling
Kosher salt and freshly ground black pepper

Puree everything in a blender. Strain. Season with salt and pepper to taste. Pop into the fridge until chilled. Serve totally chilled and garnish with extra cilantro and sriracha.

## THAI TOMATO SOUP

A **YUM** RECIPE

Picture this: tropical thunderstorms, lightning, a tiny four-table Thai restaurant, and the comfort of a spicy tomato soup. This beautiful soup, covered in a layer of cilantro, is an unexpected twist on a comforting classic inspired by that night.

*For 2 quarts soup*
   *1 quart = 2 to 3 servings*

1 quart vegetable broth
2 stalks lemongrass, peeled and cut into
   2-inch segments
8 kaffir lime leaves, torn (If you can't find
   them, some roughly chopped basil and
   lime zest will do.)
1 tablespoon chili-garlic sauce (*nam prik
   pao*)
½ teaspoon ground cumin
¼ cup fish sauce
2 garlic cloves, minced
⅓ cup roughly chopped fresh cilantro
1 tablespoon grated fresh ginger
One 28-ounce can crushed tomatoes
½ pound small shrimp, peeled and
   deveined
4 ounces cherry tomatoes, halved (about
   ¾ cup)
½ cup canned coconut milk (optional)
2 tablespoons freshly squeezed lime juice

**1.** Combine the broth, lemongrass, kaffir lime leaves, chili-garlic sauce, cumin, fish sauce, garlic, 2 tablespoons of the cilantro, and the ginger in a soup pot over medium heat and cook for 10 minutes. If you don't mind the kaffir lime leaves and lemongrass floating around, then leave them in (I did), but if you do, feel free to strain the soup at this point.

**2.** Bring the soup to a simmer. Stir in the crushed tomatoes, shrimp, and cherry tomatoes, and cook until the shrimp are just pink, about 5 minutes. Stir in the coconut milk, if using, and the lime juice, and serve hot.

**3.** Sprinkle with the remaining cilantro to garnish.

## OLD-SCHOOL POTATO-LEEK SOUP WITH CHIVE OIL AND CROUTONS

A  RECIPE

The first soup I ever loved was my mom's potato-leek soup. It doesn't look entirely special, but the flavor is eternally wonderful. Like a giant fluffy blanket wrapped around your shoulders. Most people enjoy this soup cold as vichyssoise, but it's so brilliant when warm, why even bother with it cold?

*For 2 quarts soup*
  *1 quart = 2 to 3 servings*

5 to 6 cups cleaned and chopped large
  leeks (white and pale green parts only)
2 tablespoons unsalted butter
Kosher salt and freshly ground black pepper
6 cups chicken broth, or vegetable broth
  for vegetarian option
2 pounds russet potatoes (about 3), peeled
  and diced into ½-inch pieces
2 cups cubed baguette
¼ cup snipped or chopped chives, plus
  more for garnish
¼ cup extra virgin olive oil, plus more for
  drizzling
½ to 1 cup heavy cream, depending on
  how rich you want it

**1.** Cook the leeks in the butter with a pinch of salt and pepper in a large pot over low heat for 10 minutes. Check often. Do not brown the leeks!

**2.** Add the broth and potatoes. Bring to a low simmer and cook for 20 minutes or until the potatoes are tender.

**3.** Scoop the soup mixture into a standing blender or use an immersion blender right in the pot to puree the soup. For a very smooth texture, push through a fine-mesh strainer, then return to the pot.

**4.** To make the croutons, preheat the oven to 400°F. Place the cubed bread on a baking sheet and drizzle with olive oil. Toast for 10 minutes, until golden brown.

**5.** For the chive oil, place the chives in a food processor and, while pulsing, drizzle in the ¼ cup of olive oil. Push through a fine-mesh strainer.

**6.** Five minutes before serving, add the cream and season to taste with salt. Reheat if necessary.

**7.** To serve, garnish the soup with some chive oil, chopped chives, and a few croutons.

## MOM'S SUMMER MINESTRONE

AN (MMM) RECIPE

I'm a notorious overbuyer at the farmers'
market, and this dish is my savior. I toss in every
vegetable that I don't see myself noshing on in
the next couple of days. Consider this a blueprint,
your starting point for wherever you want to
take it. The base of a good minestrone is cooked
cannellini beans and their delicious broth. Then
I layer mine with chopped tomatoes, zucchini,
and tons of super healthy kale. The best part? One
pot is enough for a no-brainer lunch all week.

*For 3 quarts soup*
   *1 quart = 2 to 3 servings*

1 cup dried cannellini beans or white
   beans if you can't find cannellini beans
8 garlic cloves
1 sprig fresh rosemary
Kosher salt
Extra virgin olive oil
1½ cups chopped yellow onion (¼-inch
   pieces)
1 cup chopped fennel (¼-inch pieces)
2 teaspoons finely chopped fresh oregano
½ cup peeled and diced carrot
½ cup diced celery
4 ounces kale
2 quarts vegetable broth
1 head broccoli, cut into bite-size florets
3 cups diced tomatoes (cut into 1-inch
   pieces; 3 or 4 tomatoes, depending on size)
1 small zucchini, quartered and sliced
   ¼-inch thick (about 1 cup)
1 to 2 tablespoons nice balsamic vinegar
   (Syrupy Modena-style is best.)
½ cup finely chopped fresh flat-leaf
   parsley, for garnish
½ cup chopped fresh basil, for garnish

**1.** In a large pot, toss the cannellini beans, 3 of
the garlic cloves, the rosemary sprig, a big pinch
of salt, and 2 quarts water. Bring to a boil over
high heat, turn down to a simmer, and cover.
Then go watch TV for 2 hours. The beans take
forever, but it's passive work, so just let them do
their thing. You want them to be tender, and not
at all crunchy.

**2.** Heat a large pot (this will be your soup pot)
over medium heat and add about 2 tablespoons of olive oil, followed immediately by
the onion and fennel. Season with a pinch of
salt and cook until the onion and fennel are a
little browned (about 10 minutes). Mince the
remaining 5 garlic cloves and add them to the
pot with the oregano. After it has browned a bit
(about a minute), add the carrot and celery.

**3.** To prep the kale, slice out the center rib of
each kale leaf, then slice the leaves into 1-inch
pieces. Add the kale to the pot along with the
cannellini beans, their cooking liquid (remove
the rosemary sprig; it's okay if the leaves fell
off), and the vegetable broth.

**4.** Bring the whole thing to a simmer for about
15 minutes. Add the broccoli, tomatoes, and
zucchini. After another 10 minutes, add the
balsamic vinegar and salt and pepper to taste.
The balsamic gives the whole thing a nice bit of
body. Garnish with the parsley and basil.

## MOST REFRESHING GREEN GAZPACHO

A  RECIPE

Loaded with herbs, a touch of spice from the jalapeño, and some sweetness from the pineapple, this soup is perfectly balanced and so *so* refreshing. Since you're not actually cooking anything, use the absolute best, ripest vegetables and herbs you can find. The quality of your ingredients will make or break a dish like this.

*For 1½ quarts soup*

> *1 quart = 2 to 3 servings*

6 cups chopped tomatoes (preferably ripe yellow or green ones)
1 tablespoon kosher salt
1½ cups chopped cucumber
¾ cup chopped yellow or green bell pepper
1 tablespoon chopped jalapeño chile
1 large radish
1 cup finely chopped fresh pineapple, plus more for garnish
Handful of fresh flat-leaf parsley
Handful of fresh cilantro
Handful of fresh basil
2 large garlic cloves
1 tablespoon extra virgin olive oil, for garnish (optional)

**1.** Toss the tomatoes with the salt and let them sit for at least 10 minutes.

**2.** In a blender, puree the tomatoes. Strain the puree and throw away the pulp.

**3.** Return the tomato puree to the blender. Add the rest of the ingredients. Puree. Chill and garnish with pineapple or olive oil.

## SPICY SHRIMP AND COCONUT SOUP AKA *TOM YUM GOONG*

A YUM RECIPE

One day I had a bunch of mushrooms left over from the farmers' market and cold air nipping at my heels, so: soup's on! These earthy little mushrooms are the perfect complement to sweet shrimp and spicy/sour broth. Plus, it's ready to eat in under 30 minutes. I can't think of a better way to beat the cold and hunger at the same time.

*For 2 quarts soup*

*1 quart = 2 to 3 servings*

1 quart chicken broth
2 stalks fresh lemongrass, tip and base
    trimmed, the rest cut into 1-inch pieces
Three 1-inch chunks fresh ginger, peeled
6 fresh kaffir lime leaves, sliced (If you
    can't find them, some roughly chopped
    basil plus lime zest will do.)
1 tablespoon fish sauce
1 cup sliced cremini or shiitake
    mushrooms
1 teaspoon chili-garlic sauce (*nam prik
    pao*)
1 garlic clove, minced
¾ pound small shrimp, peeled and
    deveined
1 cup cherry tomatoes, halved
½ cup canned coconut milk
3 tablespoons chopped fresh cilantro, for
    garnish
3 tablespoons chopped fresh basil, for
    garnish
Sliced Thai chiles (optional), for garnish

**1.** Bring the broth and 2 cups water to a boil over high heat in a medium pot. Add the lemongrass, ginger, kaffir lime leaves, fish sauce, and mushrooms and cook for 10 minutes. Add the chili-garlic sauce, garlic, and shrimp and boil for another 3 to 5 minutes, until the shrimp are cooked through and pink.

**2.** Turn down to a simmer and add the tomatoes and coconut milk. Taste to adjust the seasoning, adding fish sauce or chili sauce to taste. If it's a little too spicy, add more coconut milk to soften it.

**3.** Garnish with the cilantro, basil, and fresh chiles for extra spice.

## ULTIMATE CHOWDER: TOMATO-BASED MISTO CHOWDER

A  RECIPE

I've always been fascinated by American regional cuisine and how the same dish differs depending on where it's made. New England versus Manhattan clam chowder is a great example. One, creamy and rich; the other, hearty and full of tomatoes. The only ingredients they share are clams and potatoes, and all civility has historically ended there. In 1939, Maine passed legislation to ban tomatoes in clam chowder.

Being a Californian has afforded me total neutrality here. So I have to wonder . . . why can't chowder be both creamy *and* tomato-y? Rich *and* hearty? Enjoy this delicious mash-up of regional history in a bowl. I like to garnish mine with bacon.

*For 3 quarts chowder*
  *1 quart = 2 to 3 servings*

¾ pound fresh cherrystone clams or ⅓ cup canned
¾ pound fresh mussels or ⅓ cup canned
4 slices thick-cut bacon, diced
1 to 2 tablespoons unsalted butter
1½ cups diced yellow onion
2 garlic cloves, minced
¼ cup all-purpose flour
1 teaspoon chopped fresh thyme leaves
1 bay leaf
1 pound Yukon Gold potatoes, peeled and chopped into ½-inch cubes
⅓ cup peeled and diced carrot
⅓ cup diced celery
½ cup diced fennel
¼ teaspoon cayenne pepper
6 cups fish or chicken broth, or less if using fresh clams and/or mussels
½ cup canned tomato puree
1 pound cod, cut into 1-inch pieces
½ pound small shrimp, peeled and deveined
1 cup heavy cream, or up to 2 cups (if desired)
Kosher or sea salt and freshly ground black pepper
Minced chives, for garnish

1. If using fresh clams and/or mussels, scrub them clean, place them in a small pot, and cover with water. Bring to a boil. Cover the pot and cook them until they completely open, 5 to 10 minutes. Remove from the heat. Remove the shellfish from the pot and set aside. (Discard any unopened clams or mussels.) Strain the steaming liquid through a fine-mesh sieve or cheesecloth to catch any grit and reserve the liquid. Remove the molluscs from their shells. Measure the liquid and use it to replace that amount of broth.

**2.** Heat a 6-quart heavy pot over low heat and add the bacon. Once it has rendered a few tablespoons of fat, increase the heat to medium and cook until the bacon is a crisp, golden brown. Use a slotted spoon to transfer the bacon to a small dish and reserve until later, leaving the fat in the pot.

**3.** Add up to 2 tablespoons of the butter (you want a total of about 3 tablespoons fat) and let it melt. Add the onion and garlic, and sauté for about 5 minutes, until the onion has softened but not browned. Add the flour and stir until everything looks pasty. Add the thyme and bay leaf.

**4.** Add the potatoes, carrot, celery, fennel, cayenne, and broth. If the broth doesn't cover the potatoes, add enough water to cover them. Turn up the heat and bring to a boil, cover, and cook the potatoes vigorously for about 10 minutes, until they are soft on the outside but still firm in the center. If the broth hasn't thickened slightly, smash a few of the potato pieces against the side of the pot and cook for a minute or two longer to release their starch.

**5.** Reduce the heat to low. Add the tomato puree, fish, shrimp, shellfish, steaming broth or juice from the clams, and the reserved bacon and cook over low heat for 5 minutes. Remove the pot from the heat and allow the chowder to sit for 10 minutes (the fish will finish cooking during this time).

**6.** Gently stir in the cream and taste for salt and pepper. If you are not serving the chowder within the hour, let it cool a bit, then refrigerate. Cover the chowder after it has chilled completely.

**7.** Use a slotted spoon to mound the chunks of fish, the onion, and the potatoes in the center of large soup plates or shallow bowls, and ladle the creamy broth around. Garnish each with a sprinkling of minced chives.

## DRESSING UP BROTH AND HOMEMADE PHO

AN MMM RECIPE

On my short list of "get well soon soups" is simple beef pho. It is a hearty broth made with marrow bones, spices, some secrets no server will ever share with me, glass noodles, rare beef, and loads of fresh herbs. Avert your eyes, pho purists: I'm about to get a little sneaky.

You'll notice that I "infuse" my broth to start most of my soups. I buy a very good (but not homemade) broth, and let it simmer for a bit with whatever else I want to add. The trick is in starting off with a solid broth (low-sodium, organic, and free-range if using chicken broth) and not being afraid to go bold with ingredients. In my quick homemade pho, I add charred ginger and heady spices, giving a mild broth some real richness and kick. Don't be shy with the garnishes, either. This is a dish that is best when it's personal, so make it your own.

*For 2 quarts broth*
   *1 quart = 2 to 3 servings*

**BROTH**
2 quarts beef broth
1 yellow onion, peeled, halved, and charred (Hold over an open flame with tongs until there are burn marks.)
2-inch-section fresh ginger, charred over an open flame

1 cinnamon stick
1 star anise
2 cardamom pods
1 tablespoon coriander seeds
2 teaspoons fennel seeds
2 cloves
¼ teaspoon freshly grated ginger
1½ teaspoons fish sauce
½ yellow onion, thinly sliced
4 ounces vermicelli rice noodles
½ pound beef sirloin, cut *very* thin (Freezing it first makes slicing it much easier.)

**EXTRA GARNISHES**
Chopped green onion
Sliced jalapeño
Fresh basil leaves
Fresh cilantro leaves
Hoisin sauce
Chili-garlic sauce
Bean sprouts
Lime wedges

**1.** Combine the beef broth, charred onion, charred ginger, cinnamon, star anise, cardamom, coriander, fennel, and cloves in a pot, bring to a boil, then turn down to a simmer for 30 minutes. Turn off the heat and let it rest for another 15 minutes.

**2.** Strain into a clean pot and add the grated ginger and fish sauce. Bring to a boil and add the onion, then the noodles. Turn off the heat and add the steak (it'll cook almost immediately). Serve in large bowls with garnishes on the side.

## FULL-BLOWN TORTILLA SOUP

A **YUM** RECIPE

Growing up in Southern California, I found an abundance of tortilla soup, usually the mediocre variety. So when I sat down to create a recipe for this family favorite with my sister in mind, I knew what it had to be: spicy, thick, and full of toppings. This soup is so simple to put together and absolutely satisfying.

*For 2 quarts soup*

*1 quart = 2 to 3 servings*

### SOUP
¼ cup extra virgin olive oil
3 corn tortillas, chopped
2 cups finely diced yellow onion
2 tablespoons ground cumin
1 teaspoon ancho chile powder
1 jalapeño chile, seeded and diced
5 garlic cloves, minced
1 quart chicken broth
One 28-ounce can diced tomatoes
Kosher salt and freshly ground black pepper

### GARNISHES
¼ cup grated cheddar
¼ cup fresh cilantro leaves
2 avocados, pitted, peeled, and cubed
Shredded cooked chicken breast
Tortilla strips, fried crisp

**1.** Heat the oil in a large saucepan over medium-high heat until hot. Add the chopped tortillas and fry until crispy, 1 to 2 minutes. Add the onion, cumin, chile powder, jalapeño, and garlic. Cook until tender, about 10 minutes.

**2.** Add the chicken broth and tomatoes and cook about 45 minutes, until the flavors have developed.

**3.** Puree in batches in a blender or use an immersion blender to puree in the pot. Add salt and pepper to taste. Serve hot and add any garnishes you like.

# AL DENTE ALL THE TIME

Rustic Pasta for Any Night

Whether it's basic pantry fare, perfect for a night on the couch, or luxurious gnocchi with béchamel, pasta always has a place on my menu and is the perfect canvas for any first-time cook. When all I have are some back-of-the-fridge veggies and hot sauce, the first thing I reach for is a box of pasta from my pantry. Add some olive oil and garlic and I have a beautiful dish. It can be that simple.

## DRIED VERSUS FRESH PASTA

Many assume that fresh pasta is "better" than dried pasta, but more time in the kitchen doesn't always mean better food. Dried pasta has a history and artistry all its own. Sometimes it's the best and only choice for a hearty ragù or rich cheese sauce. On the other hand, a fresh pasta's tenderness would be the perfect counterpoint to a delicate sauce topped with a whisper of Parmigiano. Both have their place in the canon of Italian cooking, and both are awesome—just different.

## COOKING PASTA

There really isn't any secret to perfectly cooked pasta. It's all about proportions: use enough water, and it won't stick; use plenty of salt, and it'll taste great. Two good rules of thumb are to use at least four quarts of water per pound of pasta and it should be salty enough to taste like sea water.

## SAUCY OR NOT SAUCY

This is a *major* source of contention between my mom and me. Mom likes her sauce with a little pasta, while I like it Italian style, meaning the sauce just coats the pasta. The choice is yours, but all of my recipes are on the less saucy side, so if you like it like my mom, just use less pasta.

## SUPER SIMPLE PANTRY PASTA

A **YUM** RECIPE

This is the pasta you make when you need to go to the grocery store . . . and then you wait another week. It's the culinary equivalent of your "laundry day" sweatpants, except tastier and way less embarrassing. It's also the dish you serve to a group of friends and get high fives and full bellies. Butter, a little zip from the lemon and chili, and a dusting of Parmigiano are all you need. Sometimes simple is better.

*For 2 to 3 servings*

Kosher salt
8 ounces fettuccine or whatever pasta you like
2 tablespoons unsalted butter
Pinch of chili flakes
1 garlic clove, minced
Pinch of grated lemon zest
Freshly ground black pepper
½ cup grated Parmigiano, plus more for garnish (optional)
2 tablespoons extra virgin olive oil

**1.** Get a large pot of water boiling and add a small handful of salt. When it's at a full boil (large bubbles that you can hear), add the pasta and cook as per the manufacturer's instructions. When it's almost done, scoop a piece of pasta out of the water and taste it. It should be tender but firm and you should have to use your teeth to bite through it (that's where the term *al dente*, meaning "to the tooth," comes from).

**2.** Melt the butter in a sauté pan over medium heat and add the chili flakes, garlic, and lemon zest. Let the garlic barely toast (it burns super easily), then scoop the pasta straight from the pot into the pan with tongs or a pasta scoop. The water clinging to the pasta will create a light sauce. Season with salt and pepper and stir in the grated Parmigiano. Let it cook together for a minute or two, while stirring.

**3.** Toss in a bowl and top with a drizzle of olive oil and more Parmigiano if you like.

# GNOCCHI, THREE WAYS

Rolled out lightly and cooked until just done, these gnocchi are the perfect vehicle for bright and zesty marinara, velvety béchamel, or my favorite, seared crisp in brown butter and honey.

*Note:* To get the appropriately fluffy texture, a ricer or food mill should be used.

## GNOCCHI

A (WOW) RECIPE

*For 4 servings*

1 pound Yukon Gold potatoes, peeled
3 large egg yolks
¼ cup mascarpone cheese
¼ teaspoon freshly grated nutmeg
½ teaspoon fine sea salt
¼ teaspoon freshly ground black pepper
1¼ cups all-purpose flour, plus more for
    dusting board and dough
Simple Marinara Sauce (page 70),
    Béchamel Sauce (page 71), or Brown
    Butter and Honey (page 71), for serving

Potato ricer or food mill

1. Put the potatoes into a pot and add room temp (from the tap is fine) water until the potatoes are covered by 1 inch. Cover, bring to a boil over medium heat, reduce the heat, and simmer for 15 minutes or until a fork can easily be poked through them. Drain the potatoes, shaking them a bit to dry them off. Pass the potatoes through a potato ricer or food mill into a large bowl and let them cool. You should have 2 to 2½ cups.

2. Make a mound of the potatoes with a well in the middle. Add the egg yolks, mascarpone, nutmeg, salt, and pepper. Mix into the potatoes with your hands. Sprinkle ½ cup of the flour over the potatoes and gently mix it in. You want to use an extremely gentle touch here, as the more you work the dough, the tougher and gummier it'll get. Sprinkle on more flour, little by little, mixing the dough until it comes together. Pat the dough into a large ball and cut it into 4 pieces.

3. On a lightly floured surface, roll each piece of dough into a rope about ½ inch in diameter. Cut it into ½-inch-long pieces. Lightly flour the gnocchi as you cut them, then gently roll them along the tines of a fork to create ridges. Set aside on wax paper, and for your own sanity do not place one on top of the other. This creates a big, depressing mess. Allow the gnocchi to dry for about 30 minutes while you bring a pot of well-salted water to a boil.

4. Pop the gnocchi into the boiling water and cook for about 90 seconds, or until they bob up to the top. Give them about 10 seconds of bobbing at the top, so they cook through. With a slotted spoon, transfer the gnocchi to a bowl. Serve with the sauce of your choice.

Brown Butter and Honey Gnocchi

## SIMPLE MARINARA SAUCE

A 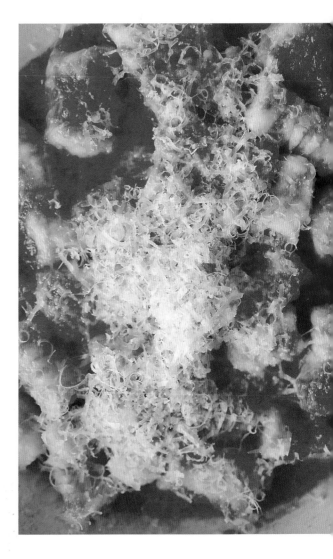

A **YUM** RECIPE

*For 2 cups sauce*

1 recipe Gnocchi (page 68)
2 tablespoons extra virgin olive oil
⅓ cup chopped onion
2 tablespoons chopped carrot
2 tablespoons chopped celery
¼ teaspoon dried oregano
One 14-ounce can whole tomatoes, with
   juice
1 garlic clove, minced
1 teaspoon kosher salt, or to taste
½ teaspoon sugar
Chopped fresh basil, for garnish
Grated Parmigiano, for garnish

**1.** In a large pot, heat the olive oil for a minute over medium heat. Add the onion, carrot, celery, and oregano and cook, stirring occasionally, until the onion is translucent but not brown. Add the tomatoes and garlic. Bring to a simmer and cook for 30 to 45 minutes, uncovered, until the sauce is slightly reduced. If you like, you can use a wooden spoon to break up the whole tomatoes while the sauce simmers.

**2.** Remove from the heat and puree in a blender or in the pot with an immersion blender until smooth. Season with the salt and sugar.

**3.** To serve, pour some sauce over the cooked gnocchi and garnish with chopped basil, if you like, and Parmigiano.

## BÉCHAMEL SAUCE

AN MMM RECIPE

*For 2 cups sauce*

1 recipe Gnocchi (page 68)
2 cups milk
2 sprigs fresh flat-leaf parsley
5 black peppercorns
½ small yellow onion, sliced
¼ teaspoon chili flakes
1 bay leaf
3 tablespoons unsalted butter
¼ cup all-purpose flour
⅓ cup grated Parmigiano
Pinch of freshly grated nutmeg
Kosher salt and freshly ground black pepper
1 teaspoon fresh thyme leaves, for garnish

**1.** Bring the milk, parsley, peppercorns, onion, chili flakes, and bay leaf to a simmer (careful not to boil the milk!).

**2.** In a separate medium pot, melt the butter over medium heat and add the flour. Whisk until doughy and smelling a bit nutty, 1 to 2 minutes, to get rid of the raw flour taste. This is your roux, or what the milk will cling to to make a sauce. Strain the milk into the roux, about a half-cup at a time, whisking to incorporate. It should be smooth and velvety, not chunky or too thick. If it is too thick, just add some more milk to thin it out. If it's too thin, turn up the heat slightly and let the sauce reduce. Whisk in the nutmeg and Parmigiano. Season with salt and pepper to taste.

**3.** To serve, pour the béchamel over the cooked gnocchi and garnish with the thyme leaves.

## BROWN BUTTER AND HONEY

A YUM RECIPE

*For 1 recipe Gnocchi*

1 recipe Gnocchi (page 68)
8 ounces (2 sticks) unsalted butter
¼ cup honey
A few drops of truffle oil (optional)
Pinch of kosher salt

**1.** Cook the gnocchi in boiling salted water for only 1 minute. With a slotted spoon, transfer the gnocchi to a bowl.

**2.** Heat a large sauté pan over medium heat and melt 1 tablespoon of the butter. Add the gnocchi (you don't want them to overlap, so you may have to do this in batches, adding a little melted butter each time). Cook the gnocchi until golden brown, and flip. Pour the gnocchi into a serving dish.

**3.** Meanwhile, in a small pot, cook the remaining butter over medium heat until barely golden brown, 3 to 5 minutes. Add the honey and continue cooking until the mixture is golden brown. Remove from the heat. If using, add the truffle oil for a lovely punch of flavor.

**4.** Drizzle the gnocchi with the sauce and season with the salt.

## SPAGHETTI WITH PEA PESTO AND RICOTTA

AN  RECIPE

My sister and mom are obsessed with peas. If it's on a menu and it's got peas in it, they will probably order it. So this pasta is for my mom and my sister, lovers of all things tasty and full of peas.

*For 2 servings*

1 cup peas (fresh or frozen)
Kosher salt
1 garlic clove
½ cup grated Parmigiano
½ cup olive oil
Freshly ground black pepper
8 ounces spaghetti or whatever pasta you
   like
½ cup ricotta

**1.** To make the pesto, first cook the peas in lightly salted boiling water until just cooked, about 1 minute. Drain and add half the peas to a food processor, reserving the other half. Add the garlic and Parmigiano to the processor. While pulsing on the food processor, drizzle in the olive oil until a loose paste forms. Taste and adjust seasoning with some salt and pepper.

**2.** Get a large pot of water boiling and add a small handful of salt. When it's at a full boil (large bubbles that you can hear), add the pasta. Cook until al dente—just done, so if the packaging says 9 to 11 minutes, aim for 9.

**3.** Add the pesto to a large sauté pan over medium heat, and cook for a minute. Scoop the pasta straight from the pot into the pan with tongs or a pasta scoop. The water clinging to the pasta will create a light sauce. Add the reserved peas and add small spoonfuls of ricotta into the sauté pan. Taste and adjust seasoning, then toss in a bowl and serve.

## ORECCHIETTE CACIO E PEPE

AN MMM RECIPE

*Cacio e pepe* literally means "cheese and pepper," and honestly, you could forgo all of the extra ingredients I included and still have a delicious dish.

*For 4 servings*

4 cups diced, peeled butternut squash
   (1-inch pieces)
1 yellow onion, halved and thinly sliced
¼ cup extra virgin olive oil
Kosher salt
10 to 12 ounces dried orecchiette
1 teaspoon freshly ground black pepper
2 tablespoons unsalted butter
2 cups torn or chopped kale (1-inch pieces)
¾ cup grated pecorino romano cheese,
   plus additional for serving
3 ounces burrata, roughly chopped

1. Preheat the oven to 425°F. Put the butternut squash and onion on a rimmed baking sheet and toss with 2 tablespoons of the olive oil and 2 teaspoons salt. Roast until tender and lightly browned, about 30 minutes, stirring once halfway through.

2. Bring a large pot of water to a boil; add 1 to 2 tablespoons salt and the orecchiette; cook al dente.

3. While the pasta is cooking, place a large sauté pan over medium heat; when the pan is hot, add the pepper and toast until fragrant, about 1 minute. Add the butter, the remaining 2 tablespoons olive oil, and the kale. Stir together until the butter melts, then remove from the heat.

4. Drain the pasta, reserving ¾ cup of the cooking water. Put the sauté pan over medium heat again. Add the pasta to the pan along with the roasted butternut squash and onion and the pecorino; toss it all together. Add some of the reserved water, a few tablespoons at a time, until the cheese melts into a creamy sauce; you might not use it all.

5. Remove from the heat and stir in the burrata. Serve with additional pecorino cheese on the side.

# BOYFRIEND SAUCE: THE PERFECT RAGÙ BOLOGNESE

A YUM RECIPE

It could just as easily be called "Girlfriend Sauce" or "I-really-care-about-you Sauce" because truly, this sauce is like a big hug. It clings to the pasta lovingly and fills your kitchen with good smells. Just let it simmer away on the stove for a few hours until the flavors and texture develop, while you watch your favorite movie in your coziest sweater with your favorite person.

*For about 8 servings*

1 pound ground beef chuck
1 pound ground pork shoulder
¼ cup diced pancetta or bacon
6 tablespoons unsalted butter
3 tablespoons extra virgin olive oil, plus
    more for serving
1 large yellow onion, finely diced
¾ cup finely diced carrot
¾ cup finely diced celery
4 garlic cloves, minced
Kosher salt
1 cup dry white wine (such as sauvignon
    blanc)
1½ cups milk
One 28-ounce can diced tomatoes
Freshly ground black pepper
1 cup beef broth (optional)
12 ounces dried tagliatelle or whatever
    pasta you like
¼ cup freshly grated Parmigiano, plus
    more for serving

**1.** Place a large pot over medium-high heat and add the beef, pork, and pancetta a third at a time, stirring and breaking up lumps with a spoon between each addition. (Adding the meat gradually allows the water to evaporate, which is key if you want to brown your meat and not boil it.) This whole process will take 15 to 20 minutes.

**2.** Turn the heat down to medium and add 4 tablespoons of the butter and the oil. Add the onion, carrot, celery, and garlic with a good pinch of salt and cook for about 15 minutes, stirring occasionally to keep it all from sticking.

**3.** Pour the white wine into the pot. With a wooden spoon, scrape up all the brown bits stuck to the bottom of your pan. These add a ton of flavor. Push the meat all around to make sure you scrape it all off. Cook for 2 to 3 minutes, to let the alcohol cook off.

**4.** Add the milk, tomatoes (with liquid), 1 teaspoon salt, and a good grinding of pepper. Bring to a boil, then lower to the lowest heat and let simmer very slowly, half covered, for 2 hours, stirring from time to time. In the end, the sauce should be more oil- than water-based, and thick like oatmeal. If it's too thick, add beef broth to thin it. Season to taste.

**5.** To put the pasta together, cook the tagliatelle in salted boiling water according to the manufacturer's instructions.

**6.** When ready to serve, mix in the remaining 2 tablespoons butter, the Parmigiano, and about ½ cup of the pasta water to the meat sauce. Drain your pasta very well and return to the pot. Add some sauce, just enough to coat the pasta. Serve with grated Parmigiano and a drizzle of olive oil.

## CLASSIC LASAGNA WITH RAGÙ BOLOGNESE, BÉCHAMEL, BURRATA, AND HERB-ROASTED TOMATOES

AN MMM RECIPE

Now that you've mastered a ragù bolognese (see Boyfriend Sauce, page 74), this is how you take it to the next level. Lasagna is the ultimate in comfort food and completely adaptable, so feel free to add in your own favorite leftovers to this decadent, crowd-pleasing dish.

*For one 9 by 13-inch baking dish of lasagna, about 12–16 servings*

### HERB-ROASTED TOMATOES
14 Roma or plum tomatoes, halved
   lengthwise
¼ cup extra virgin olive oil
Kosher salt and freshly ground black pepper
2 tablespoons fresh thyme leaves

### LASAGNA
1 pound lasagna noodles, cooked al dente
   (enough for three layers)
1 recipe Ragù Bolognese (page 74)
1 recipe Béchamel (page 71)
16 ounces burrata, chopped, or about 2
   cups chopped regular mozzarella
28 herb-roasted tomato halves
1 cup fresh basil chiffonade, lightly packed
¼ cup grated Parmigiano

1. For the tomatoes, preheat the oven to 425°F. Place the tomatoes cut side up across two baking sheets. Drizzle with the olive oil, and sprinkle with salt, pepper, and thyme. Roast for 1 hour, rotating the pans front to back halfway through. Remove from the oven and set aside to cool.

2. To put together the lasagna, reduce the oven temperature to 375°F. In a greased 9 by 13-inch baking dish, place a layer of noodles. Spread with one-third of the ragù, one-third of the béchamel, one-third of the burrata, a layer of herb-roasted tomatoes, and one-third of the basil. Repeat two times, finishing with the remaining béchamel and roasted tomatoes. Sprinkle the grated Parmigiano on top.

3. Bake for 25 minutes, or until bubbling.

4. Turn on the broiler and bake for another 5 minutes, or until brown and crunchy on top. Allow the lasagna to sit for 20 minutes before cutting into it.

## LINGUINE WITH CLAMS AND BACON

A YUM RECIPE

This is an exquisitely simple recipe and a very classic one, too. Lemon + garlic + chili + white wine + parsley + shellfish = awesome. Add bacon and pasta, and well, I mean, do I really need to explain? Feel free to take out the clams and add shrimp, scallops, or mussels, whatever makes you happy!

*For 2 to 4 servings*

1½ pounds cherrystone clams, scrubbed
    and rinsed
2 tablespoons all-purpose flour
Kosher salt
8 ounces linguine
3 slices bacon, chopped
3 garlic cloves, minced
¼ teaspoon chili flakes
Grated zest and juice of 1 lemon
1 cup white wine
2 tablespoons extra virgin olive oil
2 tablespoons finely chopped fresh
    flat-leaf parsley
Freshly ground black pepper

1. You want to purge the clams first, which just means you're making them spit out whatever sand they have left in them. Put the clams in a large bowl, cover them with cold water, and add the flour. Let them sit for 30 minutes in the fridge, and then change the water once or twice more. Rinse them off, drain them, and set them back in the fridge until you use them.

2. Bring a large pot of water to a boil, adding a small handful of salt. Cook the linguine according to the manufacturer's instructions.

3. While the pasta is cooking, in a large sauté pan over medium heat, add the chopped bacon and cook until almost crisp, 5 to 10 minutes. Add the garlic and chili flakes and cook for 30 seconds, until the garlic is lightly toasted. Add the lemon zest and clams, followed by the lemon juice and white wine. Cover the pan and cook until the clams open, about 6 minutes. Discard any unopened clams.

4. Add the linguine straight from the pot into the pan, using tongs or a pasta scoop, and mix it in with the clams. Drizzle with the olive oil, add the parsley, and season with salt and pepper.

## LAMB RAGÙ WITH MINT PESTO

AN (MMM) RECIPE

Lamb has such a beautiful, perfectly savory, and barely gamy flavor, and the meat can be easy to cook. Simmered into a simple ragù, it adds a unique twist to an otherwise traditional meat sauce. With a drizzle of mint pesto to finish it off, this is a pasta dish that plays with the classic lamb and mint combination but puts it on its head.

*For 5 servings*

¼ cup extra virgin olive oil, plus more for
    drizzling
1½ pounds ground lamb
1 yellow onion, finely chopped
1 carrot, peeled and finely chopped
1 celery stalk, finely chopped
2 garlic cloves, minced
1 teaspoon ground cumin
1 bay leaf
Kosher salt
½ cup red wine
One 28-ounce can diced tomatoes
Chicken broth or water (optional)
½ teaspoon finely chopped fresh oregano
1 pound dried pappardelle or whatever
    pasta you like
Mint Pesto (recipe follows), for serving
Grated Parmigiano, for serving (optional)

**1.** In a large sauté pan over medium heat, add 2 tablespoons of the olive oil and the ground lamb. Cook for 15 minutes or until well browned. Remove the meat and drain off the fat. To get the meat properly browned, don't overcrowd it. If your pan isn't big enough, brown the lamb in two batches.

**2.** In the same sauté pan, unwashed, add the remaining 2 tablespoons olive oil and the onion, carrot, and celery. Sauté for 10 minutes, until soft and just starting to turn golden-brown. Add the garlic, cumin, bay leaf, and 1 teaspoon kosher salt. Cook for a minute, until fragrant.

**3.** Add the red wine, turn the heat to high, and cook until the wine is reduced by half. Add the tomatoes and the lamb. Simmer on low for 1 hour, adding chicken broth or water if you like a thinner sauce. It should be about as thick as oatmeal. Stir in the oregano. Remove the bay leaf.

**4.** Bring a pot of water to a boil and add a small handful of salt. Cook the pappardelle according to the manufacturer's instructions. Drain.

**5.** To serve, dress the hot pasta in the ragù and drizzle with the mint pesto. Finish with Parmigiano if you like.

## mint pesto
*For 1 cup pesto*

½ cup fresh mint leaves, lightly packed
¼ cup fresh basil leaves, lightly packed
2 garlic cloves
¼ cup grated Parmigiano
¼ cup pine nuts
¼ cup extra virgin olive oil
Kosher salt and freshly ground black pepper

Combine the mint, basil, garlic, Parmigiano, and pine nuts in a food processor, drizzling in the olive oil slowly. Add salt and pepper to taste. Store in an airtight container in the fridge until ready to use.

## ROASTED VEGETABLE PASTA WITH WALNUT PESTO

AN (MMM) RECIPE

This is an easy "make-ahead" dish that feeds everyone and leaves leftovers for days. I call it a "kitchen sink" pasta because I put practically the entire contents of the kitchen into it. Chopped butternut squash? Sure! Leeks? Why not? Kale? Okay! It's kind of ridiculous. But the lovely thing about this pasta is that it all works together.

*For 4 servings*

3 cups diced peeled butternut squash
    (½-inch cubes)
3 cups diced peeled sunchokes (aka
    Jerusalem artichokes; ½-inch cubes)
1 fennel bulb, thinly sliced
Extra virgin olive oil
Kosher salt and freshly ground black pepper
1 leek, cleaned and chopped into ¼-inch
    pieces
2 garlic cloves, minced
6 cups roughly chopped kale (veins
    removed)
Pinch of chili flakes
1 tablespoon lemon juice
8 ounces dried pasta such as penne
½ cup Walnut Pesto (recipe opposite)
¼ cup toasted breadcrumbs (optional)

1. Preheat the oven to 425°F. On a baking sheet, drizzle the butternut squash, sunchokes, and fennel with olive oil and season with salt and pepper. Roast the fennel for 15 to 20 minutes, or until the edges turn brown, and remove from the oven. Continue to roast the sunchokes and butternut squash for another 20 to 30 minutes, flipping once. You want them to be really caramelized. Remove from the oven and set aside. You want the vegetables to be hot when you add them to the pasta, so if you need to reheat them, just pop them back into the oven at 350°F for 5 minutes.

2. In a large sauté pan over medium heat, add 1 tablespoon olive oil, then the leek. Season the leek with salt and pepper, and after 5 minutes add the garlic. Cook for another 5 minutes until the leek wilts, then add the kale. Stir in the kale so that it's coated; add more olive oil if necessary. Add the chili flakes and lemon juice and cook until the kale is just wilted, about 5 minutes.

3. Meanwhile, bring a pot of water to a boil, add a small handful of salt, and cook the pasta as per the manufacturer's instructions. In a small saucepan, heat up the walnut pesto over medium-low heat.

4. Once the pasta is cooked, add it to the sauté pan with the kale. Add the roasted vegetables and walnut pesto. Stir to combine and coat. Garnish with a sprinkle of breadcrumbs, if you like, and a drizzle of olive oil.

## walnut pesto

*For 1½ cups pesto, or more if thinned out*

¾ cup cubed sourdough bread (crusts on)
½ cup milk
1½ cups raw walnuts
3 garlic cloves
¼ teaspoon freshly grated nutmeg
¼ cup freshly grated Parmigiano
Kosher salt and freshly ground black pepper

1. Soak the bread in the milk and soak the walnuts in enough hot water to cover for 15 minutes. The bread should be soft and the walnuts should have turned the water a nutty hue. Drain the walnuts, reserving the water.

2. In a food processor, combine the bread and milk, the walnuts, garlic, nutmeg, and cheese. Pulse to chop coarsely. Add ¼ cup of the walnut water and pulse until smooth. Taste and season with salt and pepper. If you want a thinner, saucier pesto, add more of the walnut water.

# SHRIMP FRA DIAVOLO

AN (MMM) RECIPE

Time is really the star ingredient in this recipe. Letting the onions soften until almost melting in texture, the sauce simmering until reduced to a rich combination of bright white wine and tomatoes, all of those complex flavors owe their awesomeness to you catching up on your guilty pleasure show while folding laundry. Sometimes being a great home cook means letting the stove do the work. The result is a sauce filled with depth and a little heat, and plump and perfectly cooked shrimp—all soaked up by your favorite pasta or rice. So sit back, and let the stove take care of the heavy lifting. Enjoy!

*For 6 servings*

½ cup extra virgin olive oil
3 large onions, chopped
2 garlic cloves, minced
¼ teaspoon kosher salt
⅛ teaspoon freshly ground black pepper
1½ pounds raw shrimp, peeled and
   deveined
2 cups dry white wine
One 14-ounce can whole tomatoes, with
   juice
2 tablespoons tomato paste
2 cups chicken broth
Pinch of chili flakes
1 pound dried pasta (Linguine is my
   favorite for this dish.)
1 tablespoon finely chopped parsley
4 tablespoons (½ stick) butter

**1.** In a large sauté pan over medium heat, add the olive oil, onion, and garlic. Season with the salt and pepper and stir while cooking. When the onion is golden but not brown, 15 to 20 minutes, add the shrimp. Cook for about 5 minutes. The shrimp should be quite pink. Add the wine. Simmer for another 5 minutes over medium heat. Remove the shrimp from the sauce with a slotted spoon and set aside in a bowl.

**2.** Stir the tomatoes with their juices and the tomato paste into the sauce and cook for 5 minutes. Add the chicken broth and chili flakes and let simmer very slowly (over low heat) for about an hour, until the sauce is thicker and has reduced slightly.

**3.** In a large pot of boiling water, add a small handful of salt, and cook the pasta as per the manufacturer's instructions. Drain the pasta and pour it into a serving dish.

**4.** When you're ready to serve, return the shrimp to the sauce to reheat. Add the parsley and butter and stir to combine. As soon as the butter is melted, pour the sauce over the pasta and serve.

# BACHELOR PASTA: FROM BACHELOR BASIC TO EPIC

This pasta is all about personal style, creativity, and just a little bit of MacGyver. I start with its most basic iteration, a simple fresh tomato sauce with zucchini, basil, and dried pasta, and take it all the way to silken, homemade pappardelle and a simmered tomato sauce with homemade meatballs. This is a great dish to add any of your other favorite veggies to (peas, corn, butternut squash, whatever you have left over in your fridge). So whether you're a mini-fridge bachelor or a George Clooney–status bachelor, it's a delicious and dinner party–worthy meal no matter how you make it.

## THE BASIC: BACHELOR PASTA

A **YUM** RECIPE

*For 4 to 5 servings*

1 tablespoon extra virgin olive oil, plus more if desired
1½ pounds fresh Italian sausage, mild or spicy (see Note)
1 yellow onion, finely chopped
Kosher salt and freshly ground black pepper
3 tablespoons unsalted butter
3 garlic cloves, minced
3 to 4 cups halved and sliced small zucchini (about ¼-inch thick)
3 pounds ripe tomatoes, roughly chopped (I like Purple Cherokee tomatoes.)
1 bay leaf
¼ cup fresh basil chiffonade
Up to 2 cups chicken or vegetable broth (optional)
10 to 12 ounces dried pasta (Linguine or fettucine are my favorites with this sauce.)
Cheese for grating, like an Italian Parmigiano or pecorino

*Note: It's really important that it's fresh sausage from behind your butcher's counter; otherwise you won't be able to remove the casing. If you can't find fresh sausage, just slice packaged sausage into ¼-inch pieces.*

**1.** Heat a large saucepan over medium-high heat with the olive oil. Cut one end of the sausage casing and push out 1½-inch balls into the pan (it squeezes out like toothpaste, and they look like small meatballs). Do this to all the sausage and brown the balls on all sides, about

*(continued on page 88)*

10 minutes. (They might not be fully cooked through, but that's fine, as they'll continue cooking in the sauce.) Set the cooked sausage aside and drain off the fat. Don't wash the pan; you want to keep all those fabulous brown bits!

2. Add the onion, a pinch each of salt and pepper, and a tablespoon of the butter (or olive oil). Allow the onion to soften, about 15 minutes; it should be translucent and slightly brown. Add the garlic and cook for another 5 minutes. Add the sausage and zucchini, cooking for a minute or two to brown slightly. Add the tomatoes, bay leaf, and a bit of the basil (1 tablespoon). Let the whole mixture cook for about 20 minutes, until the tomatoes have reduced a bit. If the sauce thickens too much, add broth.

3. Meanwhile, bring a pot of water to a boil, add a small handful of salt, and cook the pasta as per the manufacturer's instructions. Drain.

4. Remove the bay leaf and toss the cooked pasta into the sauce. Serve with freshly grated cheese and the remaining basil.

## NEXT LEVEL: HOMEMADE SAUSAGE

AN (MMM) RECIPE

To really add a depth of flavor, I make my own Italian-style sausage to put in the sauce. You can have your butcher grind your meat, but I like grinding the spices and flavors right in on my meat grinder at home.

*For 4 to 5 servings*

1¼ pounds pork shoulder, cut into 1-inch cubes
¼ pound pancetta or bacon, cut into ½-inch pieces
2 teaspoons kosher salt
2 teaspoons sugar
2 garlic cloves, minced
2 teaspoons fennel seeds, toasted and ground
¼ teaspoon cayenne pepper
1 tablespoon grated Parmigiano
½ teaspoon freshly ground black pepper
1 teaspoon pimentón (smoked paprika)
2 tablespoons red wine vinegar
3 tablespoons milk

1 tablespoon extra virgin olive oil

1. If grinding the meat yourself, mix all the ingredients together, except the milk, until well combined. Chill in the fridge until thoroughly cold.

2. Grind on a fine setting. Mix in the milk, then lightly roll the mixture into 1½-inch-large meatballs. (If you don't have a grinder, have your butcher grind the pork and pancetta for you, then mix the other ingredients into the ground meats.)

3. Heat a large saucepan over medium-high heat with the olive oil. Brown the meatballs on all sides, cooking for about 10 minutes. (They might not be fully cooked through, but that's fine, as they'll continue cooking in the sauce.) Set the cooked sausage aside and drain off the fat. Don't wash the pan; you want to keep all those fabulous brown bits!

4. Continue to make the sauce and finish the pasta as described.

# FRESH PASTA DOUGH

AN (MMM) RECIPE

To push this hearty dish over the top, I make ribbons of fresh pasta. The tenderness is perfect with a simmered-to-perfection sauce, and it's definitely worth a try if you're in an ambitious mood.

*For 4 to 5 servings*

a standing mixer with a pasta roller and
  fettuccine cutter attachments

1½ cups all-purpose flour
2 extra large fresh eggs
2 extra large fresh egg yolks

1. Attach the dough hook to your mixer (you must use a dough hook, as paddle attachments don't actually knead the dough). Pour the flour into the mixer's bowl, and form a slight well. Add the eggs and egg yolks into the well, and start the mixer on the lowest speed. If the yolks aren't breaking, feel free to break them yourself with a fork.

2. Blend for about 3 minutes on low speed until the mixture has formed a ball on the hook. If it hasn't, and is instead sticking to the sides of the mixing bowl or crawling up past the hook, add a few teaspoons of flour and give it a few more rotations. You can also do this whole process by kneading the dough with your hands, it just takes longer.

3. Put the dough onto a floured surface and knead by hand for about 2 minutes, or until the dough is firm yet elastic. The easiest method for kneading is pushing the dough forward, folding it once, turning it 90 degrees, and repeating. This is binding and developing the gluten in the flour, to ensure elastic silky pasta dough. Cover the ball with plastic wrap and let it rest for 20 minutes.

4. This is a little time consuming, but it gets quicker each time you do it. Cut off (never tear dough) a quarter section of the dough and roll it into a ⅜-inch-thick strip. Coat lightly in flour if the dough feels sticky. Set your pasta roller on level 1, and carefully feed the dough through. Fold the dough in half, and feed through again. If ribbons form (meaning, there's a ruffle in the middle of the dough), add a little more flour. On the first setting, I usually feed the dough through once, then fold and feed the dough twice, then feed it through one final time. On the next layers (I do 1, 2, 4, and 6 on my roller) I feed it through once, fold and feed once, and then feed it through a final time. Eight is the highest setting and excellent for delicate pasta dishes such as ravioli or agnolotti, but for my fettuccine I wanted there to be something to chew on so I went with 6.

Repeat this process until all the pasta has been rolled.

5. If you are not planning on cutting your pasta right away, flour the pasta and cover the dough in wax paper. Seriously, do this. I didn't flour and chose plastic wrap instead and had to pick off dough with my fingernails and start over completely. It was one of those bizarre moments when cooking almost made me cry.

6. When you are ready to cut, place a large plate underneath the cutter so it can catch the pasta. Feed each sheet through the cutter, and lightly dust with flour to keep the dough separated. It sounds like a lot of flour, but use your judgment. If it's not sticky, no need to add flour.

7. Set aside the pasta on a floured plate for immediate use, or put in a plastic bag and keep in your fridge for up to a week.

# DIRT
# CANDY

Enjoying Vegetables Raw, Roasted,
Fried, and Any Which Way

Whether raw and perfectly seasoned or roasted and caramelized, vegetables add a wallop of flavor and balance to any plate. Most vegetables are perfect and delicious as is. That is the key to vegetables: Allow their flavor and texture to tell the story. Keep it simple. I love roasting them in a medley to bring out their sugars in deep caramel notes. I love shaving them thin and keeping them raw in salad. Vegetables can go wherever you want to take them, and I want to take them everywhere.

# VINAIGRETTES

A YUM RECIPE

Making your own vinaigrettes and dressings takes practically no effort, and means that you can customize your salads to exactly how you like them. All it requires is a little basic math: the ratio of 1 to 3. For every unit of acid (acid can be lemon or lime juice, any vinegar—basically anything that makes you suck in your cheeks), you want to add three units of oil. A unit can be a tablespoon, a cup, even a gallon if you're making salad for 300. Once you have this basic ratio down, you can crack any vinaigrette code. Keep a bottle of extra virgin olive oil and balsamic vinegar in the cupboard specifically for making vinaigrettes. Also, clean out your pantry at least once every 6 months. Vinegars and oils have a shelf life, and once they become cloudy, bitter, or just don't quite taste the same, it's time to restock.

## BASIC BALSAMIC VINAIGRETTE

This is the granddaddy vinaigrette. It can be drizzled over any salad, soup, bread, or even fresh cheese. Short of drinking it, I'm pretty sure I've tried it on almost anything (even ice cream!). It's slightly sweet with a bite, and you can completely customize it to your palate. I added a short list of some of my favorite add-ons, but as always, definitely experiment with your own, too!

*For ¼ cup vinaigrette*

1 tablespoon balsamic vinegar
3 tablespoons extra virgin olive oil
Kosher salt and freshly ground black pepper

### OPTIONAL ADDITIONS
1 tablespoon finely chopped shallot
1 teaspoon chopped fresh thyme
Pinch of chili flakes
A few drops of truffle oil
1 garlic clove, minced
1 tablespoon chopped fresh basil

Combine the vinegar, oil, and salt and pepper to taste, plus any optional additions in a small container with a lid (I just use a plastic container or an empty jar) and shake.

## MUSTARD AND LEMON VINAIGRETTE

*For ¼ cup vinaigrette*

In very close second place for "most-used concoction" in my kitchen, is this vinaigrette. I love the flavor of whole-grain mustard, and with bright lemon and some garlic, this vinaigrette is perfect on so many things, especially sandwiches. Try mixing a little into some mayonnaise the next time you have french fries. You won't be disappointed.

1 tablespoon fresh lemon juice
3 tablespoons extra virgin olive oil
1 tablespoon whole-grain mustard
½ garlic clove, minced
Kosher salt and freshly ground black pepper

Combine all the ingredients in a small container with a lid (I just use a plastic container or an empty jar) and shake.

## SPICY THAI VINAIGRETTE

*For ¼ cup vinaigrette*

I love this flavor combination with any earthy or hearty salad. The spice and brightness turn any salad from "meh" into "wow."

Juice of 1 lime
1 tablespoon fish sauce
1 garlic clove, minced
½ teaspoon grated ginger
1 tablespoon light brown sugar
¼ teaspoon sriracha sauce

Combine all the ingredients in a small container with a lid (I just use a plastic container or an empty jar) and shake.

# HEIRLOOM TOMATO–ROASTED EGGPLANT SALAD

AN (MMM) RECIPE

Sumac, a Middle Eastern spice, gives the eggplant a tart kick, and when combined with cumin and chili powder, this basic salad of tomatoes, basil, and feta takes a decidedly unexpected and delicious turn.

*For 4 to 6 servings*

4 or 5 heirloom tomatoes, cut into wedges or chopped into 2-inch sections (about 3 cups)
1 garlic clove, minced
Kosher salt and freshly ground black pepper
2 small eggplants, tops removed and sliced 1-inch thick, lengthwise
¼ cup extra virgin olive oil, plus more for drizzling
1 teaspoon sumac, or grated lemon zest if you can't find sumac
¼ teaspoon chili powder
¼ teaspoon ground cumin
¼ cup fresh basil chiffonade
2 tablespoons chopped fresh mint
Balsamic vinegar, for drizzling
1 cup diced feta (½-inch cubes)

### PITA CHIPS
1 pita, cut into 1- to 2-inch squares
¼ cup extra virgin olive oil
1 teaspoon sumac, or grated lemon zest if you can't find sumac
¼ teaspoon ground cumin
¼ teaspoon chili powder
1 garlic clove, minced
Kosher salt and freshly ground black pepper

1. Place the tomatoes in a large bowl and sprinkle with the garlic and salt and pepper.

2. Preheat the oven to 375°F. On a rimmed baking sheet, drizzle the eggplant with the olive oil and sprinkle with the sumac, chili powder, cumin, and a little salt and pepper. Roast the eggplant for 15 minutes. Flip the eggplant pieces and continue to roast for another 10 minutes or until the eggplant is tender. Remove from the oven and cool the eggplant completely.

3. While the eggplant is roasting, make the pita chips: On another rimmed baking sheet, drizzle the pita with the olive oil and season with the sumac, cumin, chili powder, garlic, salt, and pepper. Bake for 15 minutes. Flip the pita and bake for another 5 to 10 minutes, until golden brown and crisp. Transfer the pita chips to a plate and let them cool.

4. Chop the eggplant into 1-inch pieces and add to the tomatoes. Add the basil and mint, drizzle with a little olive oil and balsamic vinegar, and sprinkle with a little more salt and pepper. Stir to combine, then add the pita chips and feta. Stir a couple of times to mix together and serve.

# FUJI APPLE SALAD WITH BACON, ARUGULA, AND MAPLE-YOGURT DRESSING

A YUM RECIPE

Apple + bacon + pecans + arugula is by no means a mind-blowingly new combination. Honestly, it's up there with butternut squash + sage + brown butter in the "things that go together" culinary pantheon. But adding the maple-yogurt dressing changed something. It's creamy, it's slightly sweet—I don't really know what to compare it to. Ranch? Not really. Anyway, that's not important. What *is* important is that it tastes awesome, and you should try it.

*For 4 servings*

### MAPLE-YOGURT DRESSING
¼ cup plain whole-milk yogurt
2 teaspoons chopped fresh Italian parsley
2 tablespoons extra virgin olive oil
1 tablespoon maple syrup
2 teaspoons fresh lemon juice
1 garlic clove, pressed
Pinch of kosher salt
Pinch of freshly ground black pepper

4 slices thick-cut bacon, diced
2 Fuji apples, thinly sliced
¾ cup pecan halves
5 ounces arugula

**1.** Combine all the ingredients for the dressing in a lidded container and shake to combine.

**2.** In a pan over medium-high heat, cook the bacon until just crisp. Set aside to drain on a dish lined with a paper towel.

**3.** In a big bowl, combine the bacon, apples, pecans, and arugula. Mix with as much dressing as you like.

## QUINOA PANZANELLA SALAD

AN (MMM) RECIPE

Panzanella is the perfect summer salad. Adding nutty and slightly crunchy quinoa takes this simple side and stretches it into a hearty meal. I love snacking on this after it has sat for a day or two in the fridge. The flavors meld together beautifully and it's even more delicious.

*For 4 servings*

½ fennel bulb
Extra virgin olive oil
Kosher salt
2 cups 1-inch cubes fresh sourdough
   bread
¼ red onion, thinly sliced
1½ cups cherry tomatoes, halved
¼ cup Mustard and Lemon Vinaigrette
   (page 93)
½ cup raw quinoa
½ cup fresh basil chiffonade

1. Preheat the oven to 400°F.

2. Thinly slice the fennel (I used a mandoline) and place on a baking sheet. Drizzle with olive oil, sprinkle with salt, and roast for 20 minutes, or until golden brown and crisp at the edges. Remove from the oven and let cool.

3. Coat the sourdough cubes in olive oil, place on a baking sheet, and toast in the oven for about 10 minutes, or until golden brown. Remove from the oven and let cool slightly.

4. Dress the sourdough (warm from the oven), onion, roasted fennel, and tomatoes in a bowl with the vinaigrette and let stand for 10 minutes.

5. Cook the quinoa as per package instructions and drain. Allow to cool completely.

6. Add the quinoa and basil to the sourdough mixture and toss again.

## SHAVED BRUSSELS SPROUTS WITH MUSTARD AND LEMON VINAIGRETTE AND POACHED EGG

AN **MMM** RECIPE

I probably sound like a broken record with my "put an egg on it" mantra, but truly, few savory things aren't improved by the presence of a soft-cooked egg. It creates an instant sauce, a luxurious texture, and just adds oomph. Combined with finely shaved fresh Brussels sprouts and a zesty vinaigrette, the egg rounds out this dish and makes a meal of it.

*For 2 servings*

1 pint Brussels sprouts
1 tablespoon finely chopped parsley
1 tablespoon finely chopped or snipped
    chives
¼ cup pine nuts, toasted
3 tablespoons Mustard and Lemon
    Vinaigrette (page 93)
½ cup finely shredded Parmigiano
2 eggs, poached for 3 to 4 minutes (see
    page 29)
Extra virgin olive oil, for garnish
Kosher salt and freshly ground black pepper

**1.** Shave the Brussels sprouts about ⅛-inch thick on a mandoline or with a knife.

**2.** Mix with the parsley, chives, and pine nuts. Dress with the vinaigrette and top with the Parmigiano.

**3.** Pop the eggs on top, drizzle with olive oil, and sprinkle with salt and pepper.

## KALE SALAD WITH GREMOLATA BREADCRUMBS, PARMIGIANO, AND MUSTARD AND LEMON VINAIGRETTE

A **YUM** RECIPE

If you don't like kale salad, you've most likely experienced it tough and somewhat bitter. This is probably because the leaves weren't massaged. Yep, kale leaves need a little love. By massaging the fibrous leaves, you can turn them into something sweet, tender, and more easily digestible. It's an extra minute or two of prep, but totally transforms this dish.

*For 2 servings*

### GREMOLATA BREADCRUMBS
½ teaspoon grated lemon zest
2 slices freshly toasted bread (Sourdough or whole wheat is great.)
2 tablespoons fresh flat-leaf parsley leaves, plus more for garnish
2 tablespoons fresh mint leaves
1 garlic clove
1 ounce Parmigiano, roughly chopped
1 tablespoon extra virgin olive oil

### SALAD
5 ounces kale, stemmed and chopped into 1- to 2-inch pieces (about 8 cups by volume)
3 tablespoons Mustard and Lemon Vinaigrette (page 93)
¼ cup gremolata breadcrumbs
2 ounces finely shredded Parmigiano (about ½ cup)

**1.** For the gremolata breadcrumbs, place all the ingredients except the olive oil in a food processor. Pulse until the bread is broken down into large crumbs (about the size of peas). Drizzle in the olive oil while pulsing, until the mixture is fine crumbs.

**2.** Place the kale in a large bowl and drizzle with the vinaigrette. Massage the vinaigrette right into the kale with your fingers. After a minute or two, the leaves will start to wilt and shrink a bit. Taste the kale as you go and stop when the texture is to your liking.

**3.** Sprinkle with the breadcrumbs, top with the Parmigiano, and garnish with parsley.

## FARRO SALAD WITH ROASTED SQUASH AND POMEGRANATE

AN **MMM** RECIPE

This salad is a slam dunk. The almost creamy texture of roasted squash with the caramelized sweetness of pomegranate is so appealing, and goes great in almost any dish. Here I combined it with nutty, toasty farro, which is a whole grain similar to wheat or barley. It strikes a perfect balance of texture and flavor.

*For 3 to 4 servings*

2 cups peeled, cubed kabocha squash (or
    butternut squash or pumpkin) (1-inch
    pieces)
Extra virgin olive oil
Kosher salt and freshly ground black pepper
1 cup farro, cooked as per package
    instructions to make 3 cups and cooled
¾ cup pomegranate seeds
¼ cup finely chopped fresh flat-leaf
    parsley
¼ red onion, thinly sliced

**VINAIGRETTE**
1 tablespoon red wine vinegar
3 tablespoons extra virgin olive oil, plus
    more for drizzling
Kosher salt and freshly ground black pepper

**1.** Preheat the oven to 425°F.

**2.** On a rimmed baking sheet, drizzle the squash with olive oil and season with salt and pepper. Roast for about 30 minutes, until golden brown at the edges.

**3.** Combine the cooked farro, squash, pomegranate seeds, parsley, and onion in a large bowl.

**4.** In a small container with a lid, combine the vinaigrette ingredients, shaking to combine.

**5.** Top the farro mixture with the vinaigrette and season to taste.

## SPICY STEAK SALAD

A **YUM** RECIPE

This steak salad, seasoned with Thai flavors, and even better the next day out of the fridge, is the perfect companion to warm nights. With fresh herbs, plenty of cucumber, and a little heat from chiles and sriracha, this bright and spicy salad is an easy evening barbecue option and even better with a glass of very rich pinot noir next to it.

*For 2 to 3 servings*

½ pound flank steak
Kosher salt and freshly ground black pepper
Extra virgin olive oil, for grilling
1 large head romaine, halved
1 small fresh red Thai chile, thinly sliced
1 Japanese or Persian cucumber, thinly sliced
½ red onion, thinly sliced
¼ cup fresh basil chiffonade
¼ cup fresh cilantro leaves
2 tablespoons fresh mint chiffonade

**VINAIGRETTE**
Juice of 1 lime
1 tablespoon fish sauce
1 garlic clove, minced
½ teaspoon grated ginger
1 tablespoon light brown sugar
¼ teaspoon sriracha sauce

1. Heat a grill to high.

2. Season the steak with salt and pepper, brush with olive oil, and grill over high heat until desired doneness (4 to 6 minutes a side for medium-rare). Let the steak rest for 5 minutes, then slice and set aside.

3. Mix together the vinaigrette.

4. Just before serving, lightly brush the open face of the romaine halves with olive oil and season with salt and pepper. Grill over high heat for 30 seconds, or until you get grill marks. Chop the romaine into 1-inch slices.

5. Toss together the chile, cucumber, romaine, steak, vinaigrette, and red onion, and add the basil, cilantro, and mint. Season with salt and pepper to taste.

# ISRAELI COUSCOUS WITH SAUTÉED MUSHROOMS AND GOAT CHEESE

AN (MMM) RECIPE

I love the texture of the larger Israeli couscous, especially against creamy goat cheese and sautéed mushrooms. The flavors are surprisingly rich for a salad, and if you want to really show off your inner foodie, drizzle a tiny bit of truffle oil on top. It's practically decadent.

*For 2 servings*

2 tablespoons extra virgin olive oil
1½ cups cleaned, quartered, and chopped
   leeks (¼-inch-thick pieces)
1 garlic clove, minced
1 teaspoon finely chopped fresh thyme
1 teaspoon finely chopped fresh sage
3 cups sliced fresh shiitake or cremini
   mushrooms
1 tablespoon unsalted butter
1½ tablespoons sherry vinegar
1 cup Israeli couscous, uncooked
4 ounces fresh goat cheese
Kosher salt and freshly ground black pepper

**1.** Over medium-low heat, add 1 tablespoon of the olive oil to the pan and cook the leeks until limp, about 5 minutes.

**2.** Add the garlic, thyme, and sage, cook for 1 minute, then add the mushrooms, butter, and the remaining tablespoon olive oil. Cook for 20 minutes, stirring so the mushrooms don't burn. At the last minute, add the sherry vinegar, turn up the heat to medium-high, and let the vinegar bubble and reduce a bit, 2 to 3 minutes. Remove from the heat and let cool.

**3.** Cook the Israeli couscous as per package instructions. Drain and put into a large bowl to cool. Add the mushroom mixture to the couscous. Add the goat cheese and salt and pepper to taste, stirring gently to combine.

# GRILLED CORN SALAD WITH FETA AND BACON

AN  RECIPE

Lime, ancho chile, and cilantro, along with the grilled corn, bring *norteño* flair to this dish, while feta and bacon push it over the top. There are a lot of flavors happening, but this is a more is more situation, where everything works together.

*For 2 to 4 servings*

6 ears corn, husks and silk removed
½ cup finely chopped red onion
⅓ cup chopped fresh cilantro
1 teaspoon ancho chile powder
1 tablespoon lime juice
3 tablespoons extra virgin olive oil, plus
   more for drizzling
6 slices bacon, chopped into ¼-inch pieces
6 ounces feta, cut into 1-inch cubes
Kosher salt and freshly ground black pepper

**1.** Rub the corn with a little olive oil and sprinkle with salt and pepper. Grill over high heat (or broil in the oven), turning constantly, until the corn has some black spots and smells fragrant. Let the corn cool, then cut the kernels off the cob. Combine the corn kernels in a bowl with the red onion and cilantro.

**2.** To make the vinaigrette, combine the ancho chile powder, lime juice, and oil in a lidded container and shake together until combined. Pour over the corn mixture.

**3.** In a saucepan over medium heat, cook the bacon until crisp.

**4.** Add the feta and bacon to the corn mixture, lightly mix together, and season with salt and pepper to taste.

## SPRING POTATO SALAD WITH PEAS, MINT, AND EGGS

AN (MMM) RECIPE

Inspired by the fresh flavors of spring and my nana's classic potato salad, this is a light, fresh version, perfect for picnics and barbecues. The trick is in the balsamic vinegar, which soaks into warm potatoes, adding a depth of flavor and a slight sweet-and-sour balance. The fresh herbs, green peas, and perfectly done eggs make this the ultimate springtime salad.

*For 3 to 4 servings*

1½ pounds rose potatoes or other waxy
   potatoes, cut into 1½-inch pieces
Kosher salt
1 tablespoon balsamic vinegar
1 tablespoon extra virgin olive oil
2 eggs (preferably a few days old, for easy
   peeling), at room temperature
¼ cup finely chopped shallots
2 garlic cloves, minced
3 tablespoons mayonnaise
1 cup green peas (fresh or frozen)
1 tablespoon finely chopped chives
1 tablespoon finely chopped fresh mint
Freshly ground black pepper

1. Place the potatoes in a pot and cover with cold water (just an inch over the potatoes). Add a large pinch of salt, cover, and bring to a boil. Turn down to a simmer and cook for 5 to 10 minutes, until a fork easily goes into them. Drain the potatoes and place in a bowl. While still warm, drizzle with the balsamic vinegar and olive oil, mixing lightly to coat.

2. To hard-boil the eggs, place the eggs in a pot of cold water, just covering the eggs by 1 inch, bring to a boil, turn down to a simmer, and cook for 10 to 12 minutes. Place the cooked eggs in cold water to cool completely. Peel, cut into sixths, and set aside.

3. Add the shallots to the potatoes, then the garlic and mayonnaise.

4. Cook the peas in salted boiling water for about 3 minutes or until bright and tender. Place in ice water to cool. Drain, then add the peas to the potato mixture. Add the chives, mint, and a healthy dose of salt and pepper. Add the eggs last, as they break down easily, and gently mix together.

# LEAFY GREEN SALADS

Leafy greens are so much more than the side salads you order at dinner. Here are the ins and outs of putting together a truly fabulous green salad, whether it's with crunchy and bright romaine, soft and tender lettuce, or bitter and bold arugula.

## CRUNCHY GREENS

Crunchy greens lend themselves to fat and salt; just think of the caesar salad. So with that in mind, cover these greens with creamy dressings, pungent cheese, and even smoky bacon. If you want something easy to serve to a crowd, the fresh crispness and mild sweetness of these greens are perfect for mixing with salami, hard-boiled egg, avocado—any strong flavor or texture that can use a little brightness.

For the best, freshest texture, prep the leaves right before you plan on serving them. If you tear or cut them ahead of time, they'll lose some of their sweetness and texture.

- Romaine
- Iceberg
- Butter lettuce

## GRILLED CAESAR SALAD

AN (MMM) RECIPE

Okay, I'm getting a little attached to my grill. Leafy greens aren't the first thing I'd think would be delicious with a bit of flame under them, but the burnt bits have a wonderful nuttiness that's quite unexpected. The texture doesn't become mushy or crispy, but slightly soft, like sautéed spinach. With crunchy grilled bread and some shavings of Parmigiano, it makes the perfect rustic accompaniment to any barbecued meat. Enjoy!

*For 4 servings*

Leaves from 1 sprig rosemary, chopped
½ cup extra virgin olive oil, plus more for drizzling
1 baguette loaf
Kosher salt and freshly ground black pepper
1 garlic clove, halved
2 heads romaine lettuce, halved lengthwise
1 ounce shaved Parmigiano (I use a vegetable peeler.)

### CAESAR DRESSING
1 large egg
Juice of 1 lemon (about 2 tablespoons)
1 oil-packed anchovy fillet, drained and minced
2 garlic cloves, minced
1 tablespoon whole-grain mustard
¼ cup extra virgin olive oil
Kosher salt and freshly ground black pepper

1. Set the grill to high heat.

2. Start with the croutons, as the grilled romaine cannot be made ahead. In a bowl, mix the rosemary and olive oil. Slice the bread on the diagonal (so you get larger pieces) about 1-inch thick and brush with the olive oil mixture. Sprinkle with salt and pepper and grill until well marked on each side. Rub each piece of bread with garlic and set aside.

3. To make the dressing, whisk all the ingredients together, adding salt and pepper to taste.

4. Drizzle the romaine halves with olive oil and grill until slightly marked, 20 to 30 seconds.

5. You can serve the salad deconstructed by putting the romaine halves, grilled bread, and cheese on plates, and let dinner guests chop it up and dress it themselves. Or you can chop the romaine and bread into 1-inch pieces, and place in a bowl to toss with the dressing and some shavings of Parmigiano.

# SWEET GREENS

These are crowd-pleasing workhorse greens. Usually little salads are the culinary equivalent of beige. So boring and yet so ubiquitous. Why put up with mediocrity when something delicious is so easily within reach?

These greens can be paired with almost anything. Make a Mexican-inspired salad with avocado, corn, and a lime-cilantro vinaigrette, or maybe go Greek with briny olives, crisp cucumbers, and creamy feta. These greens are a wonderful counterpoint to bright acidic flavors, but the delicate texture means they'll wilt and crumple under the heft of heavier dressings, so light vinaigrettes all the way with these guys!

- Spinach
- Mesclun mix
- Mâche

## MESCLUN GREENS WITH AVOCADO AND HOMEMADE PITA CHIPS

AN (MMM) RECIPE

*For 2 servings*

4 ounces mesclun mix
1 cup cherry tomatoes, halved
1 cup chopped Japanese cucumber or other thin-skinned cucumber (¼-inch cubes)
1 cup Pita Chips (see Heirloom Tomato–Roasted Eggplant Salad, page 94)
2 tablespoons snipped chives
3 tablespoons Mustard and Lemon Vinaigrette (page 93)
½ cup cubed avocado

**1.** Combine the mesclun, tomatoes, cucumber, pita chips, and chives in a bowl. Add the dressing a little at a time until you're happy with the amount.

**2.** Add the avocado and stir once to combine (you want to prevent the avocado from smearing the lettuce).

# BITTER GREENS

Bitter greens are the best antidote to a high-fat dish. Pork belly or sausage practically screams out for a fresh counterpoint to all of that beautiful, golden grease.

- Arugula
- Radicchio
- Dandelion greens

## WARM BITTER GREENS WITH WALNUTS, GOAT CHEESE, AND PEAR

AN MMM RECIPE

*For 2 servings*

3 tablespoons unsalted butter
1 garlic clove, minced
1 medium head radicchio, sliced ½-inch
   thick
Kosher salt and freshly ground black pepper
1 tablespoon balsamic vinegar, plus more
   for garnish
2 ounces fresh goat cheese
1 ripe pear (preferably Bosc)
⅓ cup roughly chopped toasted walnuts
1 tablespoon extra virgin olive oil, for
   garnish

1. Melt the butter in a large sauté pan over medium heat. Add the garlic and cook for a minute or two until just golden brown. Add the radicchio, season with a little salt and pepper, and cook until wilted and slightly browned, 2 to 3 minutes. Turn off the heat.

2. Add the balsamic vinegar and goat cheese, letting it melt slightly as you stir the radicchio.

3. Divide the radicchio between two plates. Slice the pear into eighths, arrange on the salads, and garnish with the walnuts and balsamic and olive oil.

# HOW TO SERVE
# ROASTED VEGETABLES
# THREE WAYS

A ⬤YUM RECIPE

Roasted vegetables are a perfect no-brainer side. A little bit of caramelization and crisping up around the edges enhance the flavor of almost any vegetable. I pictured a few of my favorite vegetables here, but you can roast any vegetable you'd like. The only thing to be careful about is timing, as the more delicate vegetables need less time, while larger or denser ones can take quite a while. I've included three different flavor profiles for you to play with: Roasted Salsa Verde, Chimichurri, and Moroccan Spice.

## ROASTED VEGETABLES

*For 3 to 4 servings*

1½ pounds vegetables:
   Cauliflower and broccoli, cut into florets
   Butternut squash and pumpkin, peeled and
      cut into 1½-inch cubes
   Carrots, peeled, halved, and quartered
   Parsnips, peeled, halved, and quartered
   Potatoes and yams, cut into 1½-inch cubes
      or wedges, skin on or off
¼ cup olive oil
1 tablespoon kosher salt
2 teaspoons freshly ground black pepper
Roasted Salsa Verde, Chimichurri, or
   Moroccan Spice, for serving (recipes
   opposite)

1. Preheat the oven to 425°F.

2. Spread the vegetables across one or two baking sheets. You don't want the vegetables to be overcrowded, so none should be overlapping. Toss with the olive oil, salt, and pepper until fully coated. Roast for 20 to 50 minutes, depending on the vegetable (20 to 30 minutes for more delicate vegetables, 40 to 50 minutes for sturdier vegetables like potatoes). Flip twice with a spatula during cooking in order to ensure even browning. You want them golden brown at the edges and fork-tender.

3. Serve hot, with your choice of sauce.

## roasted salsa verde

*For 1½ cups sauce*

8 fresh tomatillos (see Note)
6 garlic cloves
1 tablespoon olive oil
1 poblano chile (the large dark green ones)
½ bunch fresh cilantro
2 teaspoons Mexican hot sauce, or more if
    you like it spicy
Kosher salt and freshly ground black pepper

*Note: If fresh tomatillos are not available, use the canned version, but don't roast them.*

**1.** Preheat the oven to 450°F. Unwrap and rinse the tomatillos. They're surprisingly sticky. Arrange on a baking sheet.

**2.** Place the garlic on aluminum foil, drizzle with olive oil, and close up. Place on the baking sheet with the tomatillos. Roast for 10 minutes, then remove the garlic and crank the oven up to broil. Broil the tomatillos for 5 to 7 minutes, until browned and oozing.

**3.** Using a pair of tongs, char the poblano over an open flame until the skin is black all over (or broil if an open flame isn't available). Once it has cooled, scrape off the skin, slice off the top, and remove the seeds.

**4.** Add the tomatillos, cilantro, garlic, poblanos, and hot sauce to a food processor. Blend the whole thing together. Season with salt and pepper to taste, and drizzle over the finished vegetables.

## chimichurri

*For 1 cup sauce*

½ cup fresh flat-leaf parsley leaves
½ cup fresh cilantro leaves
2 tablespoons fresh oregano leaves
3 garlic cloves
¼ cup olive oil
1 tablespoon red wine vinegar
Kosher salt and chili flakes

Blend all the ingredients to desired consistency in a food processor. (I like mine a little chunky.) Season to taste. Drizzle over the finished vegetables.

## moroccan spice

*For 1½ pounds roasted vegetables*

1 teaspoon ground cumin
½ teaspoon chili powder
½ teaspoon pimentón (smoked paprika)
⅛ teaspoon ground cinnamon
Pinch of cayenne pepper
Kosher salt and pepper
¼ cup roughly chopped fresh cilantro
½ red onion, thinly sliced

**1.** Mix together the cumin, chili powder, pimentón, cinnamon, and cayenne and sprinkle over the vegetables, along with salt and pepper, before roasting.

**2.** Once roasted, sprinkle the cilantro and red onion over the finished vegetables.

## MEXICAN STREET CORN

A  RECIPE

This corn is a can't-miss. Sweet, toasted, creamy, sour, and a teensy bit spicy all at the same time. You'll be picking kernels out of your teeth and hair for days, and your fingers will sting with chile and lime—and it's *totally worth it*. If you haven't enjoyed the bliss of blackened corn with these true Mexican flavors, well, friend, get grillin'.

*For 4 servings*

2 tablespoons vegetable oil
4 ears corn, husked, silk removed
¼ cup mayonnaise
1 cup crumbled queso fresco
Ancho chile powder
1 lime, cut into wedges
Fresh cilantro leaves, for garnish

**1.** Heat the grill to high.

**2.** Lightly oil the corn and grill until well marked by the grill. I love it almost burnt, but feel free to go a little lighter if you're not into that.

**3.** Combine the mayonnaise and queso and spread all over the grilled corn with a spatula. Dust the corn with ancho chile powder and squeeze with lime (1 wedge per cob should suffice). Sprinkle with cilantro and serve warm.

## PICKLED FENNEL

A  RECIPE

*For five or six 8-ounce jars*

1 tablespoon kosher salt
½ cup rice vinegar
½ cup apple cider vinegar
¾ cup sugar
2 cups hot water
1 large fennel bulb, thinly sliced
2 teaspoons mustard seeds
2 teaspoons coriander seeds
½ teaspoon chili flakes

5 or 6 clean mason jars

**1.** Mix together the salt, vinegars, sugar, and water in a nonreactive saucepan and bring to a simmer over medium heat, stirring until the sugar and salt are fully dissolved.

**2.** Fill the clean glass jars with the fennel, being careful not to pack it in too tightly; you want a little room for the brine to get in. Evenly distribute the spices in the jars and fill to the top with brine. Close the lids and let cool to room temperature. Keep in the fridge.

**3.** For immediate use, let it chill in the fridge for at least an hour. It's good for up to 2 weeks.

# TEMPURA-FRIED CAULIFLOWER

A **WOW** RECIPE

Unlike carrots, peas, corn, beets, and potatoes, which hold the same general flavor no matter what you do to them, cauliflower is a bit of a chameleon. Roasted with some spices, fried and served with a piquant sauce, or pureed into a creamy soup, this veggie really lends itself to transformation.

*For 2 to 3 servings*

### DIPPING SAUCE
½ cup rice vinegar
1 garlic clove, minced
1 Thai chile, thinly sliced
1 tablespoon chopped fresh cilantro
1 tablespoon sugar
¼ teaspoon kosher salt

2 quarts vegetable oil, or enough to be
  2 inches deep in your pot
1 large egg yolk
¾ cup ice water
½ cup all-purpose flour, sifted
½ teaspoon kosher salt
1 teaspoon ground cumin
1 head cauliflower, florets broken apart

*Note: The trick here is to mix together the batter at the very last second before you dunk and fry your vegetables. Make sure you're using ice-cold water, and don't overbeat the batter. Lumps are fine!*

**1.** Combine the dipping sauce ingredients in a small pot and simmer until the sugar is dissolved. Pour into a bowl and keep warm to serve with the hot tempura.

**2.** In a Dutch oven or any heavy-bottomed pot, heat the oil over medium heat until the temperature reaches 365°F, then start mixing your batter.

**3.** In a medium bowl, beat the egg yolk and mix in the ice water. Stir in the flour, salt, and cumin. Stir only until mixed; the batter will be slightly lumpy.

**4.** Dip the cauliflower into the batter using tongs or chopsticks, drain for 2 to 3 seconds over the bowl, and then add to the hot oil, which should be at 375°F. Adjust the heat to maintain between 375° and 400°F. Fry 6 to 8 pieces at a time, until puffy and very light golden, about 1 to 2 minutes. Drain on a paper towel and serve immediately with the dipping sauce.

# NOT-SO-CAPRESE SANDWICH

AN (MMM) RECIPE

There was one summer when I ate this sandwich for lunch every day. A typical caprese has fresh mozzarella with raw tomatoes and basil, and while that is always and forever a beautiful combination, I tweaked it a bit here. This is a wonderful version of the sandwich, perfect for breakfast, lunch, or maybe two slices for dinner.

*For 1 sandwich*

4 ounces cherry tomatoes
Kosher salt and freshly ground black pepper
2 tablespoons extra virgin olive oil, plus
    more for drizzling
2 slices sourdough bread (½-inch thick)
3 tablespoons ricotta
1 tablespoon fresh basil chiffonade
Balsamic vinegar, for drizzling

1. Preheat the oven to 425°F. Place the cherry tomatoes on a baking sheet lined with parchment paper or a silicone mat and sprinkle with a pinch of salt, a pinch of pepper, and the olive oil. Roast for 20 to 30 minutes, until the tomatoes are wrinkled and their bottoms are caramelized. Set aside to cool.

2. For your sandwich, you can toast the bread or not. Spread the ricotta on one slice of the bread and top with the roasted tomatoes and basil.

3. Drizzle with olive oil and balsamic vinegar, and season with salt and pepper. Serve open-faced like a tartine, or top with the other slice of bread.

## THE PERFECT AVOCADO SANDWICH WITH GARLIC AÏOLI

A **YUM** RECIPE

Creamy avocados spread on a crusty sourdough take on an almost smoky flavor, and it's a lovely complement to the heat and crunch of the garlic aïoli slaw. This is the perfect summer sandwich that will please any kind of eater.

*For 3 sandwiches*

### GARLIC AÏOLI
½ cup mayonnaise
1 tablespoon whole-grain mustard
1 garlic clove, minced
2 tablespoons finely chopped fresh flat-
    leaf parsley
Large pinch of grated lemon zest
1 tablespoon lemon juice
1 tablespoon extra virgin olive oil

6 slices sourdough bread, cut ½-inch thick
2 large avocados, halved, pitted, peeled,
    and sliced ¼-inch thick
1 large tomato, sliced ¼-inch thick
½ small head cabbage, shredded
2 carrots, peeled and shredded
1 jalapeño chile, thinly sliced (remove
    seeds to reduce heat)
Kosher salt and freshly ground black pepper

**1.** For the aïoli, combine all the ingredients in a bowl and taste to adjust the seasoning. Set aside for immediate use, or store in a container in your fridge for 2 to 3 days.

**2.** For the sandwich, toast the bread until browned.

**3.** Place one-third of the sliced avocado on each bottom slice and top with a few slices of tomato.

**4.** In a bowl, combine the cabbage, carrots, and jalapeño and dress with as much aïoli as you like. Sprinkle a pinch of salt and pepper on top of each sandwich and add a handful of the cabbage slaw. Top with the other slice of bread.

# SWEET POTATO FRIES

A **YUM** RECIPE

I usually roll my eyes at "baked" french fries.
Like nonfat cheese or pig-less bacon, I ask
myself "Why?" I've always been part of the "eat
small amounts of exactly what you like" camp
rather than the "eat a lot of this watered-down
crap" camp, but every now and then those
avenues intersect, and everyone's a winner.
Baked sweet potato fries are such an instance.

*For 2 servings*

2 large yams/sweet potatoes, not peeled
¼ cup extra virgin olive oil
½ teaspoon ground cumin
Pinch of cayenne pepper
¼ teaspoon pimentón (smoked paprika)
Kosher salt and freshly ground black pepper

**1.** Preheat the oven to 400°F. Cut the yams into
¼- to ½-inch wedges and coat with the oil.
Combine the cumin, cayenne, and pimentón
in a bowl. Sprinkle over the yams, along with
salt and pepper to taste.

**2.** Mix with your hands to coat evenly. Spread
on a baking sheet in a single layer, careful not
to crowd (even go over onto a second sheet if
you need to).

**3.** Bake until crisp, 25 to 30 minutes, flipping
once halfway through. Broil for a minute for
extra crispiness if you like. Serve immediately.

# HOMEMADE PEACH BBQ SAUCE

A (YUM) RECIPE

Peaches + rich meat make a fantastic combination in salads and sandwiches. The acid, sweetness, and savoriness all come out to play. Offset by pale ale and plenty of spice, the peaches provide a lovely back note to this BBQ sauce.

*For 2 pint jars*

8 ounces ripe yellow peaches, peeled, pitted, and chopped
2 cups ketchup
1½ cups pale ale
¼ cup Worcestershire sauce
¼ cup firmly packed light brown sugar
2 tablespoons molasses
2 tablespoons whole-grain mustard
½ teaspoon ground cumin
¼ teaspoon sweet paprika
¼ teaspoon dry mustard
½ teaspoon freshly ground black pepper

1. Combine all the ingredients in a saucepan and slowly bring to a boil over medium heat. Reduce the heat to medium-low and gently simmer until dark, thick, and richly flavored, 10 to 15 minutes. Puree with an immersion blender or ladle into a standing blender and puree.

2. Transfer the sauce to clean glass jars, cover, cool, and store in your refrigerator for up to 2 weeks.

## HOMEMADE BANANA KETCHUP

A **YUM** RECIPE

When I first encountered banana ketchup, it was at a Filipino restaurant, getting poured over my sweet sausage and rice bowls. It's pretty addicting stuff. Mildly sweet and creamy from the bananas, this isn't a Banana sauce with a capital B, but more a banana sauce, like a subjective truth rather than a philosophical absolute. The banana is the key player but not the star. It ties the sauce together, giving the ketchup its special flavor. Whether you choose to share the secret or not, I'll leave it to you.

*For 3 to 4 pints ketchup*

2 tablespoons olive oil
1 large yellow onion, roughly chopped
5 garlic cloves, chopped
¼ teaspoon ground allspice
⅛ teaspoon cayenne pepper
1½ teaspoons black peppercorns, ground
1 tablespoon ground cumin
1 tablespoon ground coriander
1 teaspoon pimentón (smoked paprika)
¼ teaspoon freshly grated nutmeg
Two 28-ounce cans whole tomatoes
2 teaspoons grated fresh ginger
2 ripe bananas, mushed with a fork
2 bay leaves
3 tablespoons apple cider vinegar
⅔ cup light brown sugar, packed
2 tablespoons kosher salt

**1.** In a large pot over medium heat, heat the olive oil and add the onion. Cook until slightly translucent, about 5 minutes. Add the garlic, allspice, cayenne, pepper, cumin, coriander, pimentón, and nutmeg and stir for a minute. Add the tomatoes, ginger, bananas, and bay leaves.

**2.** Bring to a boil, then return to a simmer for 20 minutes.

**3.** Remove the bay leaves. Puree the contents of the pot until uniform (an immersion blender makes this super easy). Add the vinegar and brown sugar to the sauce over medium-low heat. Reduce for about 20 minutes, then add the salt.

**4.** Pour into clean glass jars, cover, and cool to room temperature. Refrigerate when cool. It will keep in the fridge for up to 2 weeks.

# POTATOES FOUR WAYS

Whether perfectly crisp/never soggy home-made chips, rich and textured smashed pota-toes, the golden perfection of a dad's herbed french fries, or the ultimate in simplicity—buttery mashed potatoes—they're one of the most versatile ingredients in any kitchen.

## HOMEMADE SALT AND PEPPER POTATO CHIPS

AN **MMM** RECIPE

*For 4 servings*

4 medium russet potatoes
2 tablespoons kosher salt, plus more for
    sprinkling
2 quarts vegetable oil
1 tablespoon freshly ground black pepper

**1.** Slice the potatoes paper-thin (you'll want to use a mandoline for this) and hold them in a medium bowl of ice water with the salt mixed in. Dry them off just before adding to the oil.

**2.** Bring the oil up to 375°F in a deep, heavy pot and add the slices of potatoes, working in small batches. Stir with tongs to make sure no slices are sticking together.

**3.** Drain the chips on paper towels and sprinkle with salt and pepper while still hot. Serve immediately!

## PARMIGIANO SMASHED POTATOES

A **YUM** RECIPE

*For 4 servings*

4 medium russet potatoes
¼ cup grated Parmigiano
4 tablespoons (½ stick) unsalted butter
2 tablespoons sour cream
Kosher salt and freshly ground black pepper
1 tablespoon snipped chives, for garnish

**1.** Stab the potatoes with a fork all over and microwave on high for 10 to 15 minutes, until soft. Cut into ½-inch slices, keeping the skin on. While they're still hot, add to a bowl.

**2.** Sprinkle with the cheese, butter, sour cream, and a little salt and pepper. With a large fork or masher, smash the potatoes until the ingredients combine. Top with snipped chives.

## DAD'S FRENCH FRIES

A  RECIPE

*For 4 servings*

1 gallon vegetable oil
5 medium russet potatoes
Sea salt
A few sprigs fresh sage
A few sprigs fresh rosemary
A few sprigs fresh thyme

**1.** Heat the oil in a deep, heavy pot over medium heat until it reaches 350°F. Meanwhile, slice your russets ¼- to ½-inch thick, skin on.

**2.** When the oil is ready, add one-third of the potato slices and stir once with some tongs, just to make sure they don't clump together. Cook for about 10 minutes, until a deep golden brown.

**3.** Set aside in a tray lined with paper towels. Immediately sprinkle with sea salt. Cook the remaining fries in batches.

**4.** Add the herbs to the oil and fry for 30 seconds. Crumble the herbs on top of the potatoes and toss.

# THIS IS HOW YOU MASH POTATO

A  RECIPE

*For 4 servings*

A potato ricer or a food mill (This is what gives them a light, airy texture.)

1½ pounds Yukon Gold potatoes, peeled and quartered
½ cup heavy cream
4 tablespoons (½ stick) unsalted butter
¼ cup milk
Kosher salt and freshly ground black pepper

**1.** Put the potatoes into a pot and add room temp (from the tap is fine) water until the potatoes are covered. Cover and bring to a boil, then reduce the heat and simmer for 15 minutes, or until a fork can easily be poked through them. Drain the potatoes, shaking them a bit to dry them off.

**2.** Meanwhile, in a small pot over medium-low heat, warm the cream and melt the butter together.

**3.** Press the hot potatoes through the ricer into a bowl, or work through a food mill. Add the cream and melted butter.

**4.** Use a strong spoon to mix together, adding milk to achieve the consistency you desire. (Do not overbeat or your potatoes will get gluey.) Season with salt and pepper to taste.

# THE SAVORY

---

Indulging Your Love of All Things Meat,
Poultry, and Seafood

Cooking meat, poultry, or seafood is an intimidating threshold to pass for a first-time cook. It can be expensive and, when cooked poorly, kind of a mess. My philosophy is: Keep it simple, know what you're working with, and the results will probably be delicious. Whether it's my family's Sunday night favorite of herb-roasted chicken, or paella-inspired steamed mussels, meat, poultry, or seafood can be easy and even fun to prepare for the novice cook. All it takes is a little guidance and some confidence.

# LAMB CHOPS THREE WAYS

A **YUM** RECIPE

I *love* lamb. Love it. The slightly gamy flavor means you can take it in a ton of different flavor directions: fresh and herbaceous, bright and zesty, or earthy with a hint of spice. The other thing I love about lamb? Chops take about 6 minutes total to cook. Serve with a salad and you'll have your entire meal done in under 15 minutes. Boom. Done!

## HERB-CRUSTED

*For 2 servings*

1 pound single-rib lamb chops (about 6 chops)
1 teaspoon fennel seeds (see Note)
1 garlic clove, minced
Kosher salt and freshly ground black pepper
1 teaspoon dried oregano
1 teaspoon finely chopped fresh rosemary
Extra virgin olive oil

**1.** Let the lamb sit out on the counter while you get your ingredients together, to take the chill off from the fridge (but no more than 30 minutes).

**2.** With a mortar and pestle or spice grinder, crush the fennel seeds until well broken down. Add the garlic and a pinch of salt, and stir until a paste forms. Add the oregano and rosemary and grind to combine. Rub the mixture onto the lamb chops, then sprinkle with salt and pepper on both sides.

**3.** Heat a sauté pan over medium-high heat. When it's hot, add a drizzle of olive oil (angling the pan to coat it) and add the lamb chops. Let them cook for 2 to 3 minutes per side for medium-rare.

*Note: If you don't have a mortar and pestle or spice grinder, you can use the same amount of ground fennel.*

## MINT PESTO

*For 2 servings*

1 pound single-rib lamb chops (about 6 chops)
¼ cup fresh mint leaves, lightly packed
¼ cup fresh flat-leaf parsley, lightly packed
1 garlic clove
½ teaspoon grated lemon zest
¼ cup grated Parmigiano
¼ cup toasted pine nuts
¼ cup extra virgin olive oil, plus more for drizzling
Kosher salt and freshly ground black pepper

**1.** Let the lamb sit out on the counter while you get your ingredients together, to take the chill off from the fridge (but no more than 30 minutes).

**2.** To make the pesto, combine the mint, parsley, garlic, lemon zest, Parmigiano, and pine nuts in a food processor. While you pulse it, drizzle in the olive oil until a loose paste forms. Season with salt and pepper to taste.

**3.** Heat a sauté pan over medium-high heat. When it's hot, add a drizzle of olive oil (angling the pan to coat it) and add the lamb chops. Let them cook for 2 to 3 minutes per side for medium-rare. Drizzle with the pesto and serve.

## MOROCCAN SPICED

*For 2 servings*

1 pound single-rib lamb chops (about 6
   chops)
½ red onion, thinly sliced
1 tablespoon roughly chopped fresh
   cilantro
1 tablespoon roughly chopped fresh flat-
   leaf parsley
1 tablespoon sherry vinegar
Extra virgin olive oil
1 teaspoon light brown sugar
Kosher salt and freshly ground black pepper
1½ teaspoons ground cumin
½ teaspoon chili powder
½ teaspoon pimentón (smoked paprika)
⅛ teaspoon ground cinnamon
Pinch of cayenne pepper

**1.** Let the lamb sit out on the counter while
you get your ingredients together, to take the
chill off from the fridge (but no more than 30
minutes).

**2.** Mix together the onion, cilantro, parsley, sherry
vinegar, 2 tablespoons olive oil, the brown sugar,
and salt and pepper. Let the onion marinate for
about 10 minutes before serving.

**3.** Mix together the cumin, chili powder,
pimentón, cinnamon, and cayenne. Rub the
mixture onto the lamb chops. Sprinkle with salt
and pepper on both sides.

**4.** Heat a sauté pan over medium-high heat.
When it's hot, add a drizzle of olive oil (angling
the pan to coat it) and add the lamb chops.
Let them cook for 2 to 3 minutes per side for
medium-rare.

**5.** Pop the onion mixture on top of the lamb
chops and serve.

## HENRY'S BURGER WITH CLAIRE'S GARNISHES

A **YUM** RECIPE

I've always ground my own meat or asked the butcher to do it for me; it guarantees freshness, and I know what's going into it. My brother, Henry, takes it even deeper, taking great care to hunt down and toy with the right blend of meat. I should also mention that Henry is a burger purist: bacon, barbecue sauce, and nothing else, usually. He likes a burger that's all about the meat and bun. Here I've added some of my favorite garnishes to Henry's burger, but for all of the persnickety eaters out there, feel free to stick to Henry's simple burger.

*For 6 burgers*

**SPECIAL SAUCE**
¼ cup mayonnaise
2 tablespoons ketchup
1 tablespoon finely chopped sweet pickle
1½ teaspoons apple cider vinegar
1 teaspoon sugar

**BURGERS**
1 pound beef chuck
1 pound beef brisket
Kosher salt and freshly ground black pepper
6 slices cheddar (optional)
6 buns, halved
3 tablespoons unsalted butter
Butter lettuce leaves
6 slices bacon, cooked

**CLAIRE'S GARNISHES**
1 red onion, thinly sliced
1 tomato, sliced ¼-inch thick
2 cups arugula
Garlic Aïoli (see Perfect Avocado Sandwich, page 121)

1. To make the sauce, mix all the ingredients together. Store in the fridge until ready for use.

2. Preheat the oven to 425°F. Cube the meat and season with salt and pepper. Double grind the chuck and the brisket, or have your butcher do this for you beforehand and then season it yourself. (The fresher the grind, the better the taste and texture.)

3. Very gently, form six patties, 4 to 5 inches wide and ¾-inch thick. If you compress the meat, it won't be as juicy (this goes for pressing it down with a spatula while cooking, too).

4. Heat a sauté pan over medium-high heat, and add the patties, careful not to crowd them. Cook for 4 minutes on one side, flip, and cook for 3 minutes. Top with the cheese (if you're into that sort of thing) and pop the pan with the burgers into the oven, cooking for another 2 to 6 minutes (2 for medium-rare, 6 for medium-well).

5. Pull out the burgers and let them rest for a minute. In the meantime, pop the buns into the oven, just to warm up. Spread the warm buns with a tiny bit of butter, add a burger patty to the bottom half, top with lettuce, and spread the special sauce on the other half of the bun. Top with bacon. Press together and enjoy.

6. Or, if you want to enjoy it the way I do, top your burger with some red onion, tomato slices, and a small handful of arugula. Spread aïoli on the top bun, press together, and enjoy.

## ROOT BEER–MARINATED SKIRT STEAK SANDWICH

A YUM RECIPE

What if I could combine the lovely sweet, salty, spicy, savory flavors my little brother loves into one meal? Root beer–marinated skirt steak emerged. With a bit of sriracha for heat and sesame oil for nutty roundness, the steak caramelizes beautifully on the grill and makes for the meanest steak sandwich there is. Finally, there is something I make that my brother enjoys!

*For 10 to 12 sandwiches*

### STEAK
4 pounds skirt steak, cut into manageable
   segments (about 8 inches long)
12 ounces (1 bottle) good root beer
   (preferably one made with cane sugar)
1½ cups soy sauce
¼ cup sesame oil
2 tablespoons sriracha sauce
2 garlic cloves, minced
Kosher salt and freshly ground black pepper

### SANDWICHES (OPTIONAL)
10 to 12 ciabatta rolls, halved
Salted butter
Mayonnaise
Whole-grain mustard
Pickled Fennel (page 117)
Arugula
Avocado, pitted, peeled, and sliced ¼-inch
   thick

**1.** For the steak, combine all of the ingredients in a large bowl, cover, and marinate in the fridge for a couple of hours.

**2.** To cook, heat a grill to high. Remove the steak from the fridge at least 30 minutes ahead of time to take the chill off.

**3.** Drain the steak and pat dry. Grill for 4 minutes on each side, a minute longer per side if you prefer it more well done. Remove from the grill and cover with aluminum foil.

**4.** Let it rest for 10 minutes so it remains juicy. Cut into thin slices and serve alone, or make kick-ass steak sandwiches.

**5.** Toast the ciabatta rolls lightly and butter each half.

**6.** On the top half, spread the mayonnaise and whole-grain mustard to your liking. On the bottom, add a layer of the skirt steak slices. Top with pickled fennel, arugula, and some sliced avocado.

**7.** Close the whole thing up and slice in half.

# PERFECT STEAK

AN (MMM) RECIPE

Cooking steak has forever been on my short list of "intimidating dishes." Mostly because it can be expensive and you get only one shot. There's no turning back the clock or undoing mistakes like there is with soups, stews, and other dishes you can fuss with until they're perfect. Steak is meant to be simple, restrained, and sort of a meditation on its own savory beauty. So I adapted the technique my dad taught me: Easier than grilling, browned and crisp at the edges but juicy and tender in the center, this is the way to go. This steak takes under 15 minutes to prepare, so have the candles lit, wine breathing, and sides ready before you start cooking. And make sure your kitchen exhaust is going full blast, because this will make a lot of smoke when the steak hits the pan.

*For 2 servings (or 1 very hungry person)*

One 1-pound, 1-inch-thick rib eye steak
  (Buy the best you can and go dry-aged if
  possible; it has a deeper flavor.)
½ teaspoon kosher salt
½ teaspoon freshly ground black pepper
½ tablespoon unsalted butter
1 tablespoon extra virgin olive oil

## STEAK BUTTER
½ tablespoon unsalted butter, softened
½ teaspoon freshly ground black pepper
1 small garlic clove, minced
½ teaspoon finely chopped fresh parsley

**1.** Blot the steak dry with paper towels or a clean kitchen towel. Season with salt and pepper . Let the steak come to room temperature by letting it sit on the counter for at least 30 minutes. (If you season right before cooking, the salt will draw moisture to the surface and create steam when you're trying to sear your steak. This gives you tough, gray meat instead of golden-brown awesomeness. Letting it come to room temperature first also helps the steak's texture, since a cold steak will contract when it hits the heat.)

**2.** Move the oven rack to 6 to 8 inches away from the top and preheat the oven to broil.

**3.** In a small pot over medium heat, melt the butter and olive oil together. Set aside and let it cool down a bit.

**4.** Brush the melted butter and oil all over the steak, coating it generously on both sides and on the ends.

**5.** Place a cast-iron skillet over high heat and let it fully heat up. Use long, sturdy kitchen tongs to place the steak in the hot pan. It should sizzle immediately and give off a lot of smoke.

**6.** Cook the steak for 2 minutes, until seared deeply. Don't fuss with it! If you must, press down on the steak to deepen the sear, but don't move it around the skillet.

**7.** Take the skillet off the burner and put it in the oven. (Careful! The skillet will be very hot.) Before pushing in the rack and closing the oven door, flip the steak over using the tongs. Cook the steak in the oven for 4 minutes. (Don't forget to turn off the burner.) At this point your steak will be medium-rare. If you prefer your steak closer to medium, add 2 minutes to the oven time.

**8.** Take the steak out of the oven. Remove the steak from the pan and put it on a plate. Cover it with aluminum foil and let it rest for about 5 minutes, so the juices won't leach out when you cut into it.

**9.** While the steak is resting, mix together the steak butter.

**10.** Serve the steak with the steak butter scooped on top. Dig in!

## COCONUT-SRIRACHA FRIED CHICKEN

A (WOW) RECIPE

As an obsessive Vietnamese takeout eater, the idea of sriracha fried chicken immediately captured my imagination. And instead of the traditional buttermilk, why not go slightly sweet with coconut milk? The result is a super crunchy, flakey, golden-brown, herbaceous, and extra spicy combo that is fabulous hot or cold and sliced into an American bahn mi.

*Note: Because you bake the chicken after you fry it, this chicken is perfect for big parties. Fry the chicken ahead of time and bake it off in the oven once your guests arrive. Fresh, hot fried chicken, and so little effort.*

*For 2 to 4 servings*

1 fryer chicken (about 3 pounds), cut into 8 pieces
2¼ cups canned coconut milk
1 white onion, sliced
2 tablespoons plus ½ teaspoon sriracha sauce
2 tablespoons kosher salt
¼ cup roughly chopped herbs (basil, cilantro, kaffir lime leaves or lime peel)
2½ cups all-purpose flour
1 teaspoon freshly ground black pepper
About 4 cups canola or vegetable oil, for frying

**1.** In a large bowl (or 2 large freezer bags) combine the chicken with 2 cups of the coconut milk, the onion, 2 tablespoons of the sriracha, the salt, and chopped herbs. Refrigerate overnight.

**2.** When you're ready to fry, remove the chicken from the fridge and let it sit on the counter for 20 minutes to take the chill off.

**3.** Preheat the oven to 350°F. Stir together the flour, salt, and pepper in a very large bowl. Pour the remaining ¼ cup coconut milk and ½ teaspoon sriracha into the flour and use a fork to mix until there are only little lumps throughout. The coating will be a thick paste.

**4.** Heat 1½ inches of oil in a deep, heavy-bottomed pot or Dutch oven over medium-high heat to 365°F. Drain the chicken pieces well and discard the marinade. Thoroughly coat each piece with the coating, pressing to make it adhere to the chicken. Add the chicken to the oil 3 or 4 pieces at a time. Fry for 8 minutes, flipping to make sure the chicken isn't getting too brown. Monitor the temperature of the oil to make sure the chicken doesn't burn. Return the oil to 365°F between each batch. Keep in mind that the chicken will finish cooking in the oven.

**5.** Place the partially cooked chicken on a baking sheet while you continue frying the rest of the chicken. When all the chicken has been fried, bake the chicken for 20 minutes, until the chicken is cooked through. (You know it's done when an instant-read thermometer pushed into the chicken breasts reads 165°F.)

## THAI-STYLE CHICKEN WINGS

A **YUM** RECIPE

This is my update to my family's basic teriyaki drummette recipe, with the flavors of Thailand thrown in for a kick. Fast, delicious, and a bit spicy, these make a fantastic appetizer.

*For 2 to 4 servings*

3 tablespoons vegetable oil
3 tablespoons sriracha sauce
1 teaspoon Thai chile powder or plain chili powder
1 tablespoon fish sauce
1 tablespoon light brown sugar
½ teaspoon freshly ground black pepper
2 pounds chicken wings (tips removed) and drummettes
Chile Vinegar Sauce (recipe follows)

**1.** Create a marinade by stirring together the oil, sriracha, chile powder, fish sauce, sugar, and black pepper. Pour all but 2 tablespoons of the marinade over the chicken pieces in a freezer bag. (Reserve the 2 tablespoons for use as a sauce.) Seal the bag and let marinate in the fridge for 30 minutes.

**2.** Preheat the oven to broil. Drain the chicken and discard the used marinade.

**3.** Place the chicken pieces on the rack of a broiler pan. Broil 6 to 8 inches from the heat for about 10 minutes, then flip and broil for another 6 minutes. Remove from the oven and baste with the reserved 2 tablespoons of marinade. Serve with chili vinegar sauce.

## chili vinegar sauce

½ cup white vinegar
1 tablespoon fish sauce
1 tablespoon white sugar
10 fresh Thai chiles, thinly sliced

Combine the vinegar, fish sauce, and sugar in a small pot over medium heat, and cook until the sugar is dissolved. Add the chiles and cool to room temperature.

# THE PERFECT ROAST CHICKEN

AN  RECIPE

*For 2 to 4 servings*

**BRINE**
1 gallon water, at room temperature
½ cup kosher salt
⅔ cup light brown sugar, packed
5 black peppercorns
1 bay leaf, torn
1 chicken (3 to 4 pounds)

**BUTTER UNDER THE SKIN**
2 tablespoons unsalted butter, softened
¼ teaspoon kosher salt
¼ teaspoon freshly ground black pepper
1 garlic clove, minced
1 teaspoon whole-grain mustard
¼ teaspoon chopped fresh thyme
¼ teaspoon chopped fresh rosemary
¼ teaspoon grated lemon zest

**ON THE CHICKEN AND IN THE CAVITY**
½ head of garlic (cut crosswise)
1 sprig fresh thyme
1 sprig fresh rosemary
½ lemon
1 tablespoon extra virgin olive oil
1 teaspoon kosher salt
½ teaspoon freshly ground black pepper
3 tablespoons unsalted butter, melted

1. First, the brine. Why brine? Brining makes meat juicier. When you brine meat, the salt water softens the muscle fibers, so less water is forced out during cooking, leading to a juicier piece of meat. To make the brine, combine the water, salt, sugar, peppercorns, and bay leaf in a large container. Add the chicken so it's fully submerged and put the container in the fridge. Let it sit overnight or for at least 6 hours.

2. When you're ready to start cooking, pull out the chicken, rinse off the brine, and thoroughly dry it. (Water = steam, so the drier the chicken, the crispier the skin.)

3. Preheat the oven to 375°F. Mix together all the butter ingredients in a bowl and set aside.

4. Gently loosen the skin over the breasts and stuff the butter mixture under the skin of the bird. Stuff the garlic, thyme, rosemary, and lemon half into the cavity of the chicken. Rub the oil, salt, and pepper into the skin of the chicken thoroughly.

5. Truss the chicken. Cut about 3 feet of kitchen string. Run the center of the string under the neck to the front of the bird. Tuck the wings in as you bring the string around toward the legs, roughly following the edges of the chicken breast. Bring the ends of string down between the chicken's legs, then cross the legs. Loop the strings around the outside of the chicken "ankles" and tie in a knot. The chicken should be compact, with the legs and wings close to the body. (By trussing, the chicken will cook more evenly, preventing the dilemma of dry breast meat and undercooked dark meat.)

6. Pop the chicken into a roasting pan and into the oven. About 30 minutes in, check on the chicken. Baste it with the melted butter and pan juices.

7. After 1 hour, check the temperature of the chicken by sticking an instant-read thermometer into the thigh and baste again. If the chicken is perfectly golden brown but still needs to reach 165°F, cover the chicken in foil as it finishes cooking. Cook for about an hour and a half total or until an instant-read thermometer stuck into the thigh reads 165°F.

8. When the chicken has reached 165°F, place it on a platter, cover it with foil, and allow it to rest for at least 10 minutes. (This allows the juices to settle back into the meat and provides for a moister chicken.)

9. Snip the string and carve up the bird. Start by pulling the legs away from the body so that the joint pops up. Slice through the joint with a knife to cut off the whole legs. Cut through the joint between the thigh and drumstick to separate them. Separate one breast by slicing along the breastbone. When you hit the wishbone, pivot the knife and slice toward the wing. Slice under the entire breast to separate it from the rib cage. Repeat with the other breast. Pull the wings away from the body and slice through the joint. All done!

10. Enjoy the gluttony-induced food coma!

# CHICKEN MEATBALLS

A **YUM** RECIPE

I pair my spicy chicken meatballs with an equally spicy arrabbiata tomato sauce, which means "angry" in Italian. Topped with fresh basil, bitter arugula, pungent red onion, and of course a little Parmigiano, this dish is perfect by itself, but if you want to push it into hearty territory, serve it over some spaghetti. Add some meatballs to an Italian roll for an epic sandwich the next day.

*For 12 medium meatballs*

## MEATBALLS
½ cup fine dry breadcrumbs
½ cup finely chopped yellow onion
2 garlic cloves, minced
½ teaspoon dried oregano
¼ teaspoon cayenne pepper
¼ teaspoon sweet paprika
1 tablespoon finely chopped fresh flat-leaf parsley
½ teaspoon kosher salt
½ teaspoon freshly ground black pepper
¼ cup finely grated Parmigiano
2 teaspoons tomato paste
1 pound ground dark meat chicken
⅓ cup milk
1 egg
Olive oil, for frying

## FINISHED DISH
3 cups Arrabbiata Sauce (recipe follows)
1 bunch arugula (about 6 ounces)
½ red onion, thinly sliced
½ cup finely grated Parmigiano

1. To make sure all the ingredients are evenly distributed, in a large bowl, first mix together the breadcrumbs, onion, garlic, oregano, cayenne, paprika, parsley, salt, pepper, and Parmigiano. Add the tomato paste, chicken, milk, and egg. Gently blend everything together using your fingertips, until the mixture is uniform in texture and a little sticky. Using the palms of your hands, roll into twelve 2-inch balls. You don't want to compact the meatballs too much, or they'll be dense and dry.

2. Heat a large sauté pan over medium-high heat. Add a few tablespoons of olive oil to coat the pan, and then drop in the meatballs. Cook each side (there'll be about four sides) for 2 to 3 minutes, until a deep golden brown, 10 to 12 minutes total. It's okay if they're not cooked through, as they'll fully cook in the sauce. (If you're not cooking them in the sauce, then cook them for 12 to 15 minutes total. Refrigerate them or use right away.)

3. To finish the dish, pour the arrabbiata sauce into the pan with the meatballs. Turn the heat down to low, cover, and cook for 7 to 10 minutes, until the meatballs are fully cooked through.

4. Ladle on top of a handful of arugula in each bowl and top with red onion and Parmigiano.

## arrabbiata sauce

*For 4 cups sauce*

2 tablespoons extra virgin olive oil
2 large garlic cloves, minced
¼ teaspoon chili flakes
One 28-ounce can whole tomatoes, with
   juice
1 teaspoon tomato paste
½ cup dry white wine
1 cup fresh basil chiffonade
Kosher salt and freshly ground black pepper

**1.** In a medium saucepan over medium heat, heat the oil. Add the garlic and chili flakes. Cook for 30 seconds. Add the tomatoes and wine. Cook for 5 minutes, add ¾ cup of the basil, and cook for another 5 minutes.

**2.** Using an immersion blender (or in a blender in batches), puree the sauce. Season to taste. Add the remaining ¼ cup basil. Use immediately or store in the fridge for up to 2 weeks.

# PAELLA-INSPIRED MUSSELS

A **YUM** RECIPE

This is the perfect bowl to slurp in cold weather. Steamed mussels (or clams, if you prefer) fulfill this need with their almost smoky brininess. Combined with the rich flavors found in a Spanish paella (chorizo, saffron, and white wine), this bowl of goodness will go quickly when served to two or three. Don't forget to serve with grilled bread or herbed french fries to soak up that delicious broth!

*For 2 to 4 servings*

4 pounds mussels, debearded and cleaned (see Note)
2 tablespoons extra virgin olive oil
4 ounces dry chorizo, sliced
1 medium leek, white and tender green parts only, finely diced
1 cup finely diced yellow onion
2 garlic cloves, minced
½ cup canned diced tomatoes
¼ teaspoon saffron threads, crumbled
1 teaspoon chopped fresh thyme
1 cup dry white wine
½ lemon, sliced into rounds
2 tablespoons chopped fresh flat-leaf parsley
Freshly ground black pepper

*Note: Debearding the mussels just means pulling out the tough little fibers (known as byssal threads) poking out of their sides. You can do it with your fingers, but pliers make it easier.*

**1.** Rinse and lightly brush the mussels.

**2.** Heat the olive oil in a large heavy pot over medium heat. Add the chorizo and cook until slightly crisp. Add the leek, onion, and garlic and cook for 1 minute.

**3.** Add the tomatoes, saffron, thyme, wine, lemon slices, and 1 tablespoon of the parsley. Bring to a boil. Add the mussels. Cover the pot and cook until the mussel shells open, stirring once, 6 to 8 minutes. Discard any mussels that do not open.

**4.** Using a slotted spoon, transfer the mussels to a large shallow bowl. Boil the broth in the pot until reduced to a little over 1 cup, about 3 minutes. Season to taste with pepper. Pour the broth over the mussels, and sprinkle with the remaining tablespoon parsley.

# CILANTRO PESTO SHRIMP WITH COCONUT RICE

AN (MMM) RECIPE

As much as I love Thai food, any time I approach cooking it in my own kitchen, a maelstrom of failure follows. The main issue is that I'm not a Thai grandmother who has a catalog of ingredients at her fingertips and a kitchen that churns out this type of cooking daily. With a recipe like this, though, I can feel authentic without having to restock my entire kitchen. Coconut milk and cilantro is as exotic as it gets, but the flavors and techniques give this dish a delicious Thai twist.

*For 2 servings*

**COCONUT STICKY RICE**
About 1 cup uncooked jasmine rice
1 cup canned coconut milk
¼ cup sugar
½ teaspoon kosher salt

1 tablespoon vegetable oil
2 tablespoons Cilantro Pesto (recipe
   follows)
½ pound medium shrimp, peeled and
   deveined
¼ cup toasted shredded coconut
1 teaspoon grated lime zest
1 tablespoon basil chiffonade
2 teaspoons sugar (optional)
1 teaspoon kosher salt
Fresh cilantro, for garnish

**1.** Wash and drain the rice, then cook according to the package directions. You need 2 cups cooked rice.

**2.** While the rice is cooking, combine the coconut milk, sugar, and salt in a medium pot over medium heat. Bring to a boil, stir well to deflate the roiling foam, and remove from the heat.

**3.** When the rice is ready—soft, shiny, and forming sticky clumps—transfer it to a large bowl and pour the hot coconut mixture over it. Stir well to combine, cover, and set aside for 30 minutes for the rice to absorb the mixture. Do not refrigerate the rice (this creates mealy rice).

**4.** Heat the oil in a sauté pan over low heat. Add the pesto and stir-fry it as it sizzles gently, for about a minute; keep the heat low so as not to burn the garlic. Add the shrimp and stir-fry for 2 to 3 minutes, until pink on one side. Flip and stir in the coconut, lime zest, and basil. Add sugar, if you like, and the salt and stir to dissolve, about 2 minutes. Remove from the heat.

**5.** Scoop a large mound of the coconut rice onto a plate and place several shrimp and some of the pesto on top. Make sure to scrape up all of the crunchy bits—that's the best part! Garnish with some fresh cilantro.

## cilantro pesto

*For 2 tablespoons pesto*

½ teaspoon freshly ground white pepper
Pinch of kosher salt
1½ teaspoons vegetable oil
2 tablespoons fresh cilantro leaves, lightly
   packed
2 garlic cloves

Using a food processor or mortar and pestle, blend the ingredients together into a paste. Use immediately, or store in a container in the fridge for up to 3 days.

## BUTTERNUT SQUASH SALMON CURRY

AN (MMM) RECIPE

My best friend, Christie, shares my love of Thai food, so every time I visit her in whatever city she's in, we make a date at a Thai restaurant. One of the dishes we ate recently that has occupied a space in my mind (or stomach, I guess) was a salmon pumpkin curry. Salmon held up to the spice and coconut milk beautifully, while the pumpkin added a little bit of mild sweetness and creamy texture.

*For 4 to 5 servings*

1 butternut squash, peeled, seeded, and cut into 1½-inch cubes
2 tablespoons vegetable oil
2½ tablespoons red curry paste (store-bought or homemade; recipe follows)
1 teaspoon curry powder
½ teaspoon ground turmeric
3 garlic cloves, crushed
¼ teaspoon ground cardamom
One 14-ounce can coconut milk
½ shallot, thinly sliced
1 tablespoon light brown sugar
3 thin dried red chiles (optional)
1½ pounds salmon steaks, each cut into 2 or 3 pieces
1 lime, cut into wedges, to garnish
Handful of fresh cilantro, chopped
Cooked rice noodles or rice (optional)

**1.** Parboil the butternut squash by placing it in a large pot of boiling water. Cook for 6 to 7 minutes. Drain.

**2.** Place a large, heavy-bottomed pot or pan over medium heat. Add the oil, red curry paste, curry powder, turmeric, garlic, and cardamom. Cook for a minute, stirring vigorously, until the curry paste is fragrant. Be careful it doesn't burn.

**3.** Add 1 cup of the coconut milk, the butternut squash, and the shallot to the curry paste and bring to a boil. Boil for a few minutes, stirring well, until oil separates from the coconut mixture. Add the rest of the coconut milk, return to a boil, and again boil until the oil separates. Add the sugar and chiles if using.

**4.** Add the salmon. The salmon should be mostly submerged, with the butternut squash nestled around it. If the mixture is very thick, add water as needed. Bring back to a boil, then reduce to a simmer. Simmer for 2 minutes, then flip the salmon. Continue cooking until the salmon is fully cooked, 8 to 10 minutes.

**5.** Garnish with lime wedges and fresh cilantro, and serve with rice or noodles, if you wish.

## homemade red curry paste

*For ½ cup*

5 dried whole red chiles, roughly chopped
   (depending on how spicy you like it)
1 tablespoon chopped cilantro stems
2 teaspoons grated fresh ginger
6 garlic cloves, peeled
Two 1-inch pieces lemongrass
1 teaspoon kosher salt
1 teaspoon freshly ground black pepper
3 shallots, peeled
1 teaspoon fish sauce
3 basil leaves
1 teaspoon grated lime zest
1 tablespoon vegetable oil

**1.** Soak the dried chiles in warm water until softened, about 20 minutes. Drain, but reserve the soaking water.

**2.** Combine all the ingredients, plus a tablespoon of the chile water, in a food processor and blend until a thick, smooth paste forms, about 1 minute. Add more water if needed.

**3.** Use immediately, or store in the fridge for up to 1 week.

## NASU MISO–STYLE SALMON

A YUM RECIPE

Eggplant marinated in a miso dressing, then quickly panfried, is one of my favorite dishes off a Japanese menu. It's called *nasu miso*, and it's the perfect combination of salty, sweet, and that fifth flavor, umami. Umami means, more or less, savory. Savory in that "can't quite put my finger on it" sort of way. I love this combination of flavors with salmon, but you could switch in any other sturdy fish (halibut or black cod, for instance) or go vegetarian and make this dish with eggplant. (see Note).

*For 2 servings*

3 tablespoons mirin
2 tablespoons dry sake
½ cup white miso
¼ cup sugar
½ teaspoon kosher salt
Two 6-ounce salmon fillets, skin on
2 tablespoons vegetable oil
2 tablespoons toasted sesame seeds
¼ cup finely chopped green onions

**1.** In a small saucepan, bring the mirin and sake to a boil. Whisk in the miso until dissolved. Add the sugar and salt and cook over moderate heat, whisking, just until dissolved. Set aside and let cool.

**2.** Cover the salmon with the marinade in a container, seal, and marinate in the fridge for at least 1 hour.

**3.** Preheat the oven to 400°F. Scrape the marinade off the salmon. Brush the oil on a heavy rimmed baking sheet. Place the salmon on the baking sheet, skin side down, and roast for 10 minutes, until flaky. Transfer to plates and garnish with toasted sesame seeds and green onions.

*Note: You can easily make this dish vegetarian by switching in eggplant for the salmon. Preheat the oven to broil. Place the top oven rack 6 to 8 inches from the top. Slice 2 Japanese eggplants in half and marinate in the miso dressing for an hour. Put the eggplants cut side down on a silicone mat or parchment paper–lined baking sheet. Broil for about 3 minutes, watching carefully so they don't burn. Turn the eggplants over and cook for another 4 to 5 minutes, until the tops are golden brown and a bit bubbly. Enjoy hot, garnished with toasted sesame seeds and green onions.*

# TACOS, POR FAVOR

I love multipurpose ideas, and you can't beat four different types of meat all for the same use: tacos. Here we have the same building blocks: tortillas, cilantro, fresh cheese, and simple salsas, but they all take on completely different attitudes when paired with different kinds of straight-off-the-grill protein. Recipes include zesty *carne asada* with a sriracha glaze, grilled adobo-scented chicken, cola *carnitas* (succulent and tender pulled pork with a hint of sweetness), and *camarones al diablo*.

The recipes are ordered from the simplest to the toughest, so as you master each recipe, move on to the next for a little more of a challenge. Choose your garnishes from the following list:

**TACO GARNISHES**
White corn tortillas
Chopped red onion
Lime wedges
Cilantro
Crema or sour cream
Salsas (see page 242)
Cheese (*cotija*)
Avocado

## CAMARONES AL DIABLO

A **YUM** RECIPE

*For 10 to 15 tacos*

3 dried chiles de árbol, stems removed
½ teaspoon dried oregano
¼ teaspoon freshly ground black pepper
⅛ teaspoon cumin, whole seeds or freshly ground
3 garlic cloves, peeled

1 medium-small yellow onion, sliced into 8 rounds
⅓ cup vegetable oil, plus more for the grill
1½ tablespoons honey
1 tablespoon lemon juice
2 tablespoons thinly sliced green onion
¼ cup hot sauce (optional)
½ teaspoon kosher salt
1½ pounds small shrimp, peeled and deveined
3 tablespoons butter, melted

**1.** In a dry pan over medium-high heat, combine the dried chiles, oregano, black pepper, and cumin. Cook for 1 to 2 minutes, until the spices are fragrant.

**2.** Combine the contents of the pan with 1 cup water and the garlic, yellow onion, oil, honey, lemon juice, green onion, hot sauce (if using), and salt in a food processor. Puree until smooth. Pour over the shrimp in a freezer bag and marinate in the fridge for at least an hour.

**3.** To cook, grease the grill and heat to medium-high. Pop 12-inch wooden skewers into water while the shrimp are marinating so they don't burn on the grill (or use metal skewers). Wipe most of the marinade off the shrimp and stick onto the skewers, about 10 per skewer, depending on the size of the shrimp. Cook for 1 to 2 minutes per side, just until the shrimp are pink and firm. Brush with butter and take off the skewers. Serve alone or in a taco.

**4.** If you don't have a grill, or just don't feel like grilling, brush off most of the marinade, heat a pan over medium-high heat, add the butter and then the shrimp (no skewers needed). Cook for 1 to 2 minutes per side, until pink and firm.

**5.** To serve, warm tortillas over an open flame, fill with shrimp, and garnish with whatever you like.

## CARNE ASADA WITH SRIRACHA GLAZE

AN (MMM) RECIPE

*For 10 to 15 tacos*

**GLAZE**

3 tablespoons vegetable oil
3 tablespoons sriracha sauce
1 teaspoon ancho chile powder
1 tablespoon fish sauce
1 tablespoon light brown sugar
½ teaspoon ground cumin
½ teaspoon freshly ground black pepper

½ bunch fresh cilantro, finely chopped
½ white onion, sliced
½ jalapeño chile, thinly sliced
4 garlic cloves, minced
½ teaspoon ground cumin
¼ cup lime juice
½ cup canola or vegetable oil, plus more
    for the grill
2 pounds skirt or flank steak
1 tablespoon kosher salt
2 teaspoons freshly ground black pepper

**1.** Combine the glaze ingredients in a bowl; give it a taste and add more chile powder or sriracha sauce if you like it spicier.

**2.** In a separate bowl, combine the cilantro, onion, jalapeño, garlic, cumin, lime juice, and oil. Add the steak and marinate, covered, in the fridge for at least 1 hour or up to overnight.

**3.** Heat the grill to medium-high and brush the grates with a little oil. Take out the steak, brush off the marinade, and rub on the salt and pepper. Let it sit out while the grill is heating, to take the chill off.

**4.** Grill for 2 to 4 minutes on each side (depending on thinness) for medium-rare. Cook 30 seconds longer for each next stage of doneness (medium, medium-well, well done). In the last minute, brush the glaze on each side.

**5.** Let the steaks rest off the heat for at least 5 minutes to seal in the juices. Slice the steak across the grain, on a diagonal. Enjoy on a plate or in a taco with your choice of garnish!

## ADOBO-SCENTED GRILLED CHICKEN

AN (MMM) RECIPE

*For 10 to 15 tacos*

**GLAZE**

⅔ cup apricot jam
2 tablespoons finely chopped shallot
2 tablespoons rice vinegar
1 tablespoon adobo sauce from canned
    chipotle chiles

½ bunch fresh cilantro, finely chopped
½ medium white onion, sliced
4 garlic cloves, minced
2 teaspoons adobo seasoning: combine
    equal parts cumin, cayenne pepper,
    dried oregano, and ancho chile powder
¼ cup lime juice
½ cup canola or vegetable oil, plus more
    for drizzling
2 pounds skin-on, boneless chicken
    breasts and thighs
2 teaspoons kosher salt
2 teaspoons ground black pepper

1. Combine the glaze ingredients in a bowl. Give it a taste and add more adobo sauce if you like it spicier.

2. Combine the cilantro, onion, garlic, adobo seasoning, lime juice, and oil in a bowl. Add the chicken. Let it marinate in the fridge for at least an hour or up to overnight.

3. Heat the grill to medium-low. Set the chicken out to take the chill off.

4. Rub off the marinade and rub in the salt and pepper. Drizzle with a little oil, brush the grill with a little oil, and place the chicken skin side down. Grill with the hood down for 10 to 12 minutes on each side. For the last minute of cooking, brush each side of the chicken with the glaze.

5. Take the chicken off the heat and let it rest for at least 5 minutes.

6. Slice the chicken into thin slices or bite-size chunks. Enjoy on a plate or in a taco with your choice of garnishes.

## COLA CARNITAS

A **WOW** RECIPE

*For 10 to 15 tacos*

2 pounds boneless pork shoulder, trimmed
   of excess fat, cut into 5-inch chunks
1 tablespoon coarse sea salt
¼ teaspoon ground cinnamon
¼ teaspoon ground allspice
1 teaspoon ancho chile powder
½ teaspoon ground cumin
2 tablespoons canola or vegetable oil
Two 12-ounce bottles Mexican cola or any
   cola sweetened with cane sugar
3 garlic cloves, peeled and smashed
1 bay leaf
1½ tablespoons apple cider vinegar

1. Preheat the oven to 350°F.

2. Rub the pieces of pork shoulder all over with the salt, cinnamon, allspice, chile powder, and cumin. Heat the oil in a Dutch oven over medium-high heat. Cook the pork in a single layer until very well browned, turning the pieces as little as possible so they get nice and dark before flipping them around, about 5 minutes per side. Cook in batches if there's not enough room.

3. Once it's all browned, pour in about a cup of water, scraping the bottom of the pan to get all the tasty brown bits. Add the cola and, if needed, a little water so the pork pieces are mostly submerged in liquid. Add the garlic and bay leaf.

4. Braise in the oven, uncovered, for 2 hours, turning the pork a few times during cooking, until much of the liquid has evaporated and the pork falls apart when poked with a fork.

5. Remove the pan from the oven (but leave the oven on) and lift the pork pieces out of the liquid, setting them on a plate. Discard the left-over liquid, garlic, and bay leaf.

6. Once the pork pieces are cool enough to handle, shred them into bite-size pieces using your hands or a fork. Taste a piece and add a sprinkling of salt if necessary. Return the pork pieces to the Dutch oven, sprinkle with the vinegar, and stir to combine. Cook in the oven until the pork is crispy and caramelized, about 15 minutes. I like mine extra crispy and crackly, so I keep it in there a little longer.

7. Enjoy on a plate or in a taco with the garnishes.

# EPIC PORK CHOP

A **WOW** RECIPE

Pork chops can go from succulent, juicy, and amazingly savory to cardboard in just a few moments. The trick all comes down to temperature. A perfectly cooked chop should be 140°F inside, slightly pink, and visibly juicy. How do you get such perfection? Here are a few tips.

1. Brine! Brining your meat helps keep the moisture in and seasons it from the inside out.

2. Go thick. It's a lot easier to control the temperature of the meat with thicker cuts. Thinner cuts cook quickly, so they're easy to overcook.

3. Rest. Let your meat rest for at least 15 minutes before cutting into it. This is to make sure all the juices stay in the meat. Cut into it too soon, and they'll drain right out.

4. Buy good meat. I got real fancy and bought heritage pork, which has a deep, savory flavor and absolutely gorgeous fat. It may sound strange, that the fat can be gorgeous, but it can and is when you buy good pork. Factory-farmed pigs have been bred to produce very lean meat, which can be dry and bland when cooked; heritage breeds tend to be fattier and thus more flavorful. Happy, well-fed animals produce the best-tasting meat, so if you can find organic, vegetarian-fed, hormone-free, small-farm-raised pork, go for it.

*For 4 servings*

### BRINE
¼ cup kosher salt
1 tablespoon light brown sugar, packed
5 whole black peppercorns
1 quart water

One 4-chop pork rib rack, with excess fat trimmed and bones frenched (excess meat is trimmed from them; have your butcher do this.)

### RUB
2 teaspoons kosher salt
1 teaspoon fresh thyme leaves
1 teaspoon crushed black peppercorns

### FINISHED DISH
2 tablespoons unsalted butter
1 teaspoon fresh thyme leaves

**1.** Combine the brine ingredients and pour into a freezer bag or container with the pork. Pop into the fridge and marinate for 1 hour or up to 2 hours.

**2.** Remove the pork from the brine; discard the brine. Rinse the pork under cold running water to reduce saltiness; pat dry with paper towels. Place the pork on a rack set over a sheet of foil in a roasting pan; let stand at room temperature while your oven preheats to take the chill off (up to 30 minutes).

**3.** Position a rack in the center of the oven and preheat to 400°F. Mix the salt, thyme, and peppercorns in a small bowl; sprinkle the rub over the pork. Roast for 40 minutes, or until an instant-read thermometer inserted into the meat reads 140°F.

**4.** Remove from the oven. Let the roast rest for 30 minutes.

**5.** Slice apart the chops. Heat a large sauté pan over medium-high heat. Melt the butter, add the thyme, and immediately add the pork chops. Sear until golden brown on both sides, about 2 minutes a side. Place on a plate with your favorite side. Enjoy!

# OUT OF THE OVEN

The How-To's of
Homemade Baking

Baking can sometimes feel like an advanced chemistry course. The measurements matter, but the more you bake, the more comfortable you get. Plus, bring a dozen muffins anywhere and people love you. I wish someone had told me that in high school. I would have been *way* more popular. You're bound to win "most popular" in everyone's hearts with these knockout recipes.

# CHOCOLATE SABLÉ CARAMEL BITES

AN (MMM) RECIPE

My friend Jonathan is a chocolatier—which, as you'd imagine, is a great friend to have. One day he popped over and I had a failed caramel–chocolate ganache tart sitting on the counter. The caramel was too loose, and everything was gooping everywhere. We went at the remnants with a fork and I asked him what he thought. "Amazing, just lose the chocolate. Oh, and more sea salt." He always wants more sea salt. So I took his advice, and here's what I created.

*For 15 sandwich cookies*

6 ounces (1½ sticks) unsalted butter, softened
½ cup white sugar, plus more for sprinkling
¼ cup light brown sugar, packed
1½ cups all-purpose flour, plus more for rolling
½ cup unsweetened cocoa powder
½ teaspoon kosher salt
2 teaspoons pure vanilla extract
½ cup grated or finely chopped bittersweet chocolate
2 cups Caramel Sauce, cold (recipe follows)
2 tablespoons coarse sea salt

1. Using a stand mixer fitted with a paddle, cream together the butter and sugars at medium speed until pale and fluffy. Sift together the flour, cocoa, and kosher salt and add to the mixer bowl gradually at a low speed. Add the vanilla and chocolate and blend until the dough becomes a rich, dark brown. Wrap the dough tightly in plastic wrap and refrigerate for 30 minutes. (The dough will keep, wrapped in plastic, for up to 1 week in the refrigerator or 3 months in the freezer.)

2. While the dough is chilling, preheat the oven to 350°F. Line a baking sheet with parchment paper or a silicone mat.

3. Roll out the dough into a rectangle ½-inch thick on a lightly floured work surface. Using a ruler, square the edges as much as possible. Using a sharp knife or a pizza cutter, cut the dough into thirty 1½-inch rectangles. Place them 2 inches apart on the baking sheet.

4. Sprinkle lightly with sugar. Bake for 15 minutes or until firm. Cool completely on a rack.

5. Spread the flat bottom of 15 of the cookies with about 2 teaspoons cold caramel sauce, sprinkle with the sea salt, sandwich with another cookie, and serve immediately. If serving later, keep in the fridge.

## caramel sauce

*For 1 cup sauce*

½ cup white sugar
4 tablespoons (½ stick) unsalted butter
6 tablespoons heavy cream
½ teaspoon pure vanilla extract

1. Melt the sugar in a medium pot over medium heat, until it turns golden. Stir with a whisk until all the sugar is dissolved and just starting to turn a lovely amber color.

2. Turn the heat to low and add the butter bit by bit, stirring to combine. Careful, it'll foam up. Add the cream and vanilla extract, stirring to combine. It'll take quite a bit of stirring, but the sauce will come together. Turn up the heat to medium and continue cooking until it's thick and syrupy, about 10 minutes.

3. Pour the caramel into a heat-resistant mason jar and let it cool to room temperature. Cover and store in the fridge for up to 2 weeks.

# BEER BROWNIES

A **YUM** RECIPE

Beer brings a lightness to these brownies that makes them unlike any others you've had. The deep, rich flavors of stout or porter are perfect with chocolate, but if beer isn't your thing, cold coffee is a delicious substitute.

*For one 9 by 13-inch baking dish; about 2 dozen brownies*

1 cup all-purpose flour
½ teaspoon kosher salt
¼ cup unsweetened cocoa powder (I used Valrhona brand cocoa.)
3½ ounces semisweet chocolate
8 tablespoons (1 stick) unsalted butter
½ cup stout or other dark beer, or cold coffee
4 large eggs, at room temperature
1 cup white sugar
1 cup light brown sugar, packed
2 teaspoons pure vanilla extract
1 cup semisweet chocolate chips

**1.** Preheat the oven to 350°F. Butter and flour a 9 by 13-inch baking dish.

**2.** Sift together the flour, salt, and cocoa.

**3.** Melt the chocolate in a heatproof bowl over a pot of boiling water. In a small pan over medium heat, melt the butter until it just turns golden brown, about 5 minutes. Pour the brown butter into the chocolate, scraping the pan to get the brown bits. Add the beer to the butter-chocolate mixture.

**4.** Using a stand mixer, beat together the eggs and sugars until thick and shiny, about 2 minutes. Continue beating on low while adding the flour mixture and chocolate mixture alternately. Finish with the vanilla. Do not overmix. Fold in the chips. Pour into the baking pan. Bake for 40 to 45 minutes, until the edges are firm and the center is set. Cool completely in the pan, then slice and serve. To store, cover the pan with plastic wrap and keep on the counter for up to a week.

## BLUE RIBBON COOKIES

A  RECIPE

I'll tell you a shameful secret. I've never been in love with my chocolate chip cookie recipe. They're efficient and delicious but not the earthshaking Cookie Monster craze-inducing disks of joy I want. So after much tinkering, I came up with a new, improved recipe. And these truly hit the mark. They are indulgent, rich, buttery, a perfect ratio of chewy to crunchy, and most important, *chocolatey.*

*For 3 dozen cookies*

8 ounces (2 sticks) unsalted butter, browned (see Brown Butter–Butternut Squash Soup, page 47) and cooled
2 cups dark brown sugar, packed
½ cup white sugar
2 large eggs, at room temperature
1 tablespoon pure vanilla extract
2½ cups all-purpose flour
1 teaspoon baking powder
1 teaspoon baking soda
½ teaspoon kosher salt
1 tablespoon instant espresso powder
1½ cups semisweet chocolate chips, or semisweet chocolate cut into chunks

**1.** Preheat the oven to 360°F. (Not a typo; 360°F is the secret temperature for my aunt's delicious chocolate chip cookies.)

**2.** Using a stand mixer fitted with a paddle, mix the butter with the sugars at medium-high speed until combined, about a minute. Add the eggs one at a time, beating until fully mixed in. Beat in the vanilla. Mix until pale, 2 to 3 minutes.

**3.** In a separate bowl, sift together the flour, baking powder, baking soda, salt, and espresso powder. Beat into the butter mixture at low speed until just incorporated. Add the chocolate chips and continue beating until mixed.

**4.** Line a baking sheet with parchment paper or a silicone mat. Drop medium balls (about 1½-inch diameter) of cookie dough onto the baking sheet about 3 inches apart. (There's enough dough for 3 batches. Let the baking sheet cool between batches.) Bake for 13 to 15 minutes, until nicely browned around the edges. The cookies will still be a bit gooey in the center.

**5.** Allow to cool for a minute or two on the baking sheet, then transfer to a cooling rack. Serve a little warm or save for later in a lidded container on the counter.

# LAVENDER SHORTBREAD COOKIES

A  RECIPE

The next time you sit down for a cup of afternoon tea, I would suggest pairing one of my favorites, Earl Grey, with lavender shortbread. The mellow earthiness of the lavender works beautifully with the bergamot notes of the tea.

*For 2 dozen cookies*

8 ounces (2 sticks) unsalted butter, softened
½ cup white sugar
¼ cup light brown sugar, packed
2 large eggs, at room temperature
1½ teaspoons dried lavender flowers (food grade only), crushed
1½ teaspoons pure vanilla extract
2 cups all-purpose flour, plus more for kneading and rolling
½ teaspoon baking powder
¼ teaspoon kosher salt
2 tablespoons crystal sugar or other decorative sugar, for garnish

**1.** Using a stand mixer fitted with a paddle, beat the butter and white and brown sugars at medium speed with the paddle until light and fluffy, 2 to 3 minutes. Add one of the eggs, the lavender, and vanilla and beat until blended.

**2.** In a separate bowl, whisk together the flour, baking powder, and salt. Add the flour mixture to the butter mixture and beat on low until just incorporated. Transfer the dough to a lightly floured work surface, knead a few times to bring it together, and then divide the dough in half. Wrap each half in plastic wrap and refrigerate until firm, at least an hour.

**3.** Preheat the oven to 350°F and place a rack in the center of the oven. Line two baking sheets with parchment paper or silicone mats.

**4.** Remove one portion of the dough from the refrigerator and place on a lightly floured work surface. Roll out the dough until it is ¼-inch thick. Using a lightly floured 2-inch round fluted cookie cutter, cut out cookies. Place them on the prepared baking sheet. Refrigerate the baking sheet of cut-out cookies for 15 to 20 minutes to chill the dough. Repeat rolling, cutting, and chilling the other half of dough.

**5.** Reroll the trimmings to ¼-inch thick, cut out cookies, and repeat until all the dough is used up

**6.** In a small bowl, whisk the remaining egg for egg wash. Remove the cookies from the refrigerator, brush the tops with the egg wash, and sprinkle with crystal sugar. Bake the cookies for 10 to 15 minutes or until golden brown around the edges.

**7.** Place the cookies on a cooling rack. Store in a container on your counter for up to a week.

# FRENCH BREAKFAST PUFFS

A  **YUM** RECIPE

Imagine if some mad scientist crossbred a muffin and a donut, dipped it in butter and rolled it in cinnamon sugar. Well, then you'd have a French Breakfast Puff. These little muffin-y donuts (or maybe it's donut-y muffins?) don't look like much when they pop out of the oven, but *wow*. These are so simple and so amazingly delicious. Please, please, pretty please give these a try!

*For 8 puffs*

5⅓ tablespoons (⅔ stick) unsalted butter, softened
1 cup white sugar
1 egg, at room temperature
1½ cups all-purpose flour
1½ teaspoons baking powder
½ teaspoon kosher salt
¼ teaspoon freshly grated nutmeg
1½ teaspoons ground cinnamon
½ cup milk
1 teaspoon pure vanilla extract
6 tablespoons unsalted butter, melted

**1.** Preheat the oven to 350°F. Grease eight cups of a muffin tin.

**2.** Using a stand mixer fitted with a paddle, beat together the softened butter and ½ cup of the sugar until fluffy, 2 to 3 minutes. Add the egg, mixing together. Sift together the flour, baking powder, salt, nutmeg, and ½ teaspoon of the cinnamon. Mix the sifted ingredients into the sugar-egg mixture alternately with the milk at low speed. Add the vanilla last, mixing to blend together.

**3.** Fill the muffin tin cups two-thirds full. Bake until barely golden brown, 25 minutes.

**4.** Immediately loosen the puffs from the tin (use a butter knife around the edges first). Working very quickly, dip the puffs into the melted butter, then roll in a mixture of the remaining sugar and cinnamon. Serve hot, at once—but honestly, these are still delicious the next day!

# BANANA-NUTELLA MUFFINS

A  RECIPE

If you're not already sold just on their name, one of the intriguing things about this recipe is the buttermilk component. It gives the muffins a little tang and depth, an excellent foil to the mellow and sweet banana. The chocolate chips and walnuts are completely optional but so, so, so good.

*For 2 dozen muffins (2 pans needed)*

2 cups all-purpose flour
1 tablespoon unsweetened cocoa powder
1 teaspoon baking soda
½ teaspoon kosher salt
8 tablespoons (1 stick) unsalted butter
1 cup white sugar
2 large eggs, at room temperature
¾ cup Nutella
½ cup buttermilk
1 teaspoon pure vanilla extract
2 cups mushed bananas (about 5 very ripe bananas)
1 cup chocolate chips (optional)
1 cup walnuts or hazelnuts, roughly chopped (optional)

**1.** Preheat the oven to 350°F. Line the cups of a muffin tin with paper liners.

**2.** Sift together the flour, cocoa, baking soda, and salt. Using a stand mixer fitted with a paddle, or a hand mixer, cream the butter and sugar together until fluffy. Add the eggs one at a time, then blend in the Nutella.

**3.** Working at a low speed, add the sifted ingredients and buttermilk alternately, ending with the buttermilk. Add the vanilla and mix together. Fold in the bananas and the chocolate chips and nuts, if using.

**4.** Pour into the muffin tin cups. Bake for 20 minutes. The doneness is mostly a "look" thing, because if you spear one, you'll probably get melted chocolate or gooey banana. The muffins should be a deep golden brown and bounce back if you push into them.

**5.** Place the muffins on a cooling rack and let them cool to room temperature. Store in a container on the counter for up to a week.

# CHOCOLATE CAKE DARK AND LIGHT*

A (WOW) RECIPE

This is one of my family's official cakes. We have it every other birthday (it seems to switch off with our other favorite, the Australian dessert Pavlova on page 198). It's also a very polarizing cake: half of my family *loves* it and the other half, the Pavlova half, well . . . doesn't. I'm on the loving half. How you couldn't love velvety soft überchocolate cake with fluffy marshmallow-y frosting is a mystery to me. Maybe it's this difference that makes birthdays such divisive, uncomfortable holidays. I kid. We love each other as much as we love our respective cakes.

And for the marshmallow frosting unbelievers, I also included a rich and decadent Dark Chocolate Buttercream Frosting for the most chocolately chocolate cake.

*toasted marshmallow
 icing or dark chocolate
 buttercream frosting

## CHOCOLATE CAKE

*For 1 double-layer 9-inch cake*

4 ounces (1 stick) unsalted butter, plus
   more for the pan
7 ounces dark chocolate, chopped
½ cup unsweetened cocoa powder (I used
   Valrhona brand)
1¾ cups all-purpose flour
½ teaspoon kosher salt
2 teaspoons baking soda
1½ teaspoons baking powder
3 large eggs, room temperature
1¼ cups white sugar
¼ cup light brown sugar, packed
2 teaspoons pure vanilla extract
½ cup sour cream
Toasted Marshmallow Icing (page 174)
Dark Chocolate Buttercream Frosting
   (page 175)

**1.** Preheat the oven to 325°F and butter two
9-inch round cake pans.

**2.** Melt the chocolate and butter in the top of a
double boiler. Add ½ cup water and the cocoa
powder. Stir until the cocoa is dissolved. Set
aside to cool.

**3.** In a medium bowl, sift together the flour, salt,
baking soda, and baking powder.

**4.** Using a stand mixer fitted with a paddle
attachment, beat the eggs for a few seconds to
combine. Add the sugars and whip at medium
speed until pale and very thick, 3 to 4 minutes.
Add the vanilla and beat for another minute.

**5.** Gently fold the chocolate mixture and sour
cream into the eggs and sugar. Fold in the flour
mixture in thirds.

**6.** Fill the pans. Bake for 25 to 30 minutes, until
a toothpick inserted into the center comes out
clean.

**7.** Cool in the pans for about 15 minutes. Turn
out of the pans onto a cooling rack. Cool completely before icing or frosting.

## toasted marshmallow icing

*For 1 double-layer 9-inch cake*

4 large egg whites
3 cups superfine sugar
½ cup plus 2 tablespoons cold water
¼ teaspoon cream of tartar
1 tablespoon light corn syrup
1 teaspoon pure vanilla extract
butane torch

**1.** Mix the egg whites, sugar, water, cream of tartar, and corn syrup in a large heatproof bowl. Fill a medium saucepan about two-thirds full with water and bring to a simmer. Place the bowl over the saucepan. (It should be about an inch away from the water.) Beat continuously with a hand mixer for 10 minutes.

**2.** At this point it should be white and thickened. Remove from the heat and beat in the vanilla. Continue beating until the icing becomes shiny, very thick, and spreadable, 10 to 15 minutes more. It needs to be very stiff to hold up the whole cake, so make sure that when the beater is pulled out of the bowl, the icing forms stiff peaks.

**3.** To ice the cake, place one cake layer on the serving dish. Put a large dollop of icing in the middle and spread it outward. The icing should be about 1 inch thick and evenly spread. Gently

place the other layer on top, careful not to push down (you don't want to squeeze out the icing). Using the same method as before, put a large dollop on the top of the cake and work your way out, spreading any excess to the sides. Keep adding icing until there is a 1-inch layer surrounding the entire cake. For aesthetics, try to spread the icing in a back-and-forth motion, creating ripples and peaks all over the cake. This improves the look of the cake if you intend on toasting it, as the torch will have more to cling to as you go over the cake. Always use what looks like an ungodly amount of icing. Better to have too much than too little and accidentally scraping chocolate cake into the white icing—I've been there, and it sucks.

**4.** To toast, get your butane torch going (you can get these at any kitchen supply store) and move it across the top of the cake from about 4 inches away, not staying in one spot for longer than 3 seconds. The cake should look like a giant toasted marshmallow: golden brown overall, with some extra toasty bits on the edges.

## dark chocolate buttercream frosting

*For 1 double-layer 9-inch cake*

1 pound 2 ounces (4½ sticks) unsalted
   butter, softened
6 cups powdered sugar, plus more to taste
3 tablespoons agave nectar or maple syrup
1½ cups unsweetened cocoa powder
1 tablespoon pure vanilla extract
½ teaspoon kosher salt

### GARNISH
2 ounces bittersweet chocolate, grated

**1.** Add the butter to a stand mixer fitted with a paddle attachment and beat until it's soft and smooth. At low speed, add the powdered sugar, mixing until fully incorporated. Add the agave nectar, cocoa powder, vanilla, and salt. Beat until smooth and uniform in texture. Taste for sweetness and add more powdered sugar if necessary.

**2.** To ice the cake, place one cake layer on the serving dish. Put a large dollop of buttercream in the middle and spread it outward. The buttercream should be about 1 inch thick and evenly spread. Gently place the other layer on top, careful not to push down (you don't want to squeeze out the buttercream). Using the same method as before, put a large dollop on the top of the cake and work your way out, spreading any excess to the sides. Keep adding buttercream until there is a 1-inch layer surrounding the entire cake. For aesthetics, try to spread the icing in a back-and-forth motion, creating ripples and peaks all over the cake. Always use what looks like an ungodly amount of buttercream. Better to have too much than too little. Top with the grated chocolate.

## TINA'S MANGO CAKE

A (WOW) RECIPE

Tina and her cakes, Tina and her pies, Tina and her cookies: It's hard for me to imagine my aunt Tina without picturing a baked good. This simple buttermilk cake with heaps of whipped cream, fresh mango, and a citrus-laden orange frosting is so unusual, and so wonderful.

*For 1 double-layer 9-inch cake*

### CAKE
3 cups all-purpose flour
1 tablespoon baking powder
½ teaspoon kosher salt
8 ounces (2 sticks) unsalted butter, softened
1¾ cups white sugar
4 large eggs, at room temperature
1 tablespoon pure vanilla extract
1 cup buttermilk

### MANGO WHIPPED CREAM
1½ cups heavy whipping cream
2 tablespoons white sugar
1 teaspoon pure vanilla extract
1½ cups chopped mango

### FROSTING
8 ounces cream cheese, softened and totally room temperature
8 ounces (2 sticks) unsalted butter, softened and totally room temperature
Pinch of kosher salt
1 teaspoon pure vanilla extract
1 teaspoon grated orange zest
¼ cup orange juice
2 cups powdered sugar
½ cup toasted coconut flakes

**1.** Preheat the oven to 350°F. Place a rack in the center of the oven. Grease two 9 by 2-inch round cake pans. Line the bottoms of the pans with parchment or wax paper, then grease the paper.

**2.** In a bowl, sift together the flour, baking powder, and salt. In the bowl of a stand mixer fitted with a paddle attachment (or with a hand mixer), beat the butter until soft and creamy. Gradually add the sugar and beat until light and fluffy, 2 to 3 minutes. Add the eggs one at a time, beating well after each addition. Add the vanilla and beat until combined. With the mixer on low speed, alternately add the flour mixture and the buttermilk, beginning and ending with the flour.

**3.** Evenly divide the batter between the two prepared pans, smoothing the tops. Bake for 25 to 35 minutes, until a toothpick inserted into the center of the cake comes out clean and the cake springs back when pressed lightly in the center.

**4.** Place the cakes on a wire rack to cool, in their pans, for about 10 minutes. Then invert the cakes onto a greased wire rack. Remove the paper and reinvert the cakes so the tops are right side up. Cool completely before frosting.

**5.** For the whipped cream, while the layers are cooling, whip the cream, sugar, and vanilla with a whisk or hand mixer until soft peaks form. Fold in the mango.

**6.** For the frosting, cream the cream cheese and butter with a stand mixer fitted with a paddle attachment until light and a little fluffy, 1 to 2 minutes. Careful not to overbeat! Add the salt, vanilla, and orange zest and juice and beat until combined. Turn the mixer to low and add the powdered sugar.

**7.** Spread the top of one layer of cake with the mango whipped cream. Sandwich the other layer of cake on top. Smooth the cream cheese frosting just on top of the top layer, and sprinkle with the coconut.

## BAKED DONUTS WITH GLAZE

AN  RECIPE

The thing about donuts is that they're basically
fried bread. Cake or yeast, it doesn't matter;
nine times out of ten, those bad boys are fried
before being dipped in a glaze or rolled in
sugar. But frying can be a hassle, so I created a
baked version that tastes just as good as the real
thing. Promise.

## DONUTS

*For 1 dozen donuts*

⅓ cup canola oil, plus extra for brushing
    the trays
¾ cup white sugar
1¼ cups all-purpose flour
1½ teaspoons baking powder
½ teaspoon kosher salt
⅛ teaspoon baking soda
1 large egg, at room temperature
½ cup buttermilk, at room temperature
2 tablespoons pure vanilla extract
¼ teaspoon freshly grated nutmeg
Cinnamon sugar, for sprinkling (optional)
Dark Chocolate Glaze (recipe follows,
    optional)
Cream Cheese Glaze (recipe follows, optional)
Salted Dulce de Leche (recipe follows,
    optional)

**1.** Preheat the oven to 350°F. Grease two
6-mold donut pans and set aside.

**2.** In a medium bowl, whisk together the sugar,
flour, baking powder, salt, and baking soda.

**3.** In a separate bowl, whisk together the oil,
egg, buttermilk, vanilla, and nutmeg. Add to the
dry ingredients a little at a time and continue
mixing with a rubber spatula, just until the
ingredients are combined.

**4.** Using a melon baller or tablespoon, drop
2½ tablespoons of batter into each mold.
Spread the batter evenly around the mold.

**5.** Bake for 10 minutes, rotate the pans front to
back and switch their positions, and bake until
the donuts are golden brown, about 10 minutes
more. Let the donuts cool in the pans for 5 minutes if sprinkling with toppings such as cinnamon sugar, 15 minutes if using glaze or icing.

In a small saucepan, bring the cream to a simmer. In a heatproof bowl, combine the 3 ounces of chopped chocolate with the corn syrup. Pour the hot cream over the chocolate and let stand until melted, about 5 minutes. Whisk until smooth. Let the glaze cool until thick but still pourable, about 5 minutes.

## cream cheese glaze
*For 1½ cups glaze*

4 ounces (1 stick) unsalted butter
1 cup white sugar
4 ounces cream cheese, at room
   temperature

Combine all the ingredients in a small saucepan with ¼ cup water over medium heat. Stir until the sugar is fully dissolved and the cream cheese is fully incorporated. Let the glaze cool until thick but still pourable.

## salted dulce de leche
*For 1 cup, plus a little more*

One 14-ounce can sweetened condensed
   milk
1 teaspoon kosher salt

Remove the label from the can of condensed milk. Poke a small hole in the top with a can opener (to release pressure so the can doesn't burst) and place it in a pot of cold water, with the water just coming up to the top edge of the can. Boil for 2 hours, adding water as it evaporates to more than halfway down the can. Remove the can and let it cool a bit. Open it and stir the salt into what is now a thick golden syrup.

**6.** Run a knife around the donuts in the molds, lift them out, and place them on a baking sheet. Coat the tops with your choice of topping.

## dark chocolate glaze
*For 1 cup glaze*

⅔ cup heavy cream
3 ounces dark chocolate, chopped (about
   1 cup)
1 tablespoon corn syrup

## BRIOCHE CINNAMON BUNS WITH CREAM CHEESE GLAZE

AN (MMM) RECIPE

Once you master this basic recipe for rich brioche bread, making these cinnamon rolls with cream cheese glaze is a snap. Be prepared to wake up out of your food coma coated in crumbs, cinnamon, and sticky glaze—these are indulgently good.

*For 8 large buns*

2¼ teaspoons active dry yeast (one ¼-ounce packet)
¼ cup white sugar
⅓ cup plus 1 tablespoon lukewarm milk
2¼ cups all-purpose flour, plus more for rolling
¼ teaspoon kosher salt
1 large egg, at room temperature
4 ounces (1 stick) unsalted butter, melted, plus more for greasing the bowl and brushing on top

### FILLING AND GLAZE
4 tablespoons (½ stick) unsalted butter, melted, plus more for greasing the pan and brushing on top
¾ cup white sugar
2 tablespoons ground cinnamon
1 recipe Cream Cheese Glaze (page 179)

**1.** Mix the yeast and sugar with the lukewarm milk in the bowl of a stand mixer with a dough hook attachment. Let it sit a few minutes while the yeast bubbles and foams up.

**2.** Add the flour and salt and mix together at medium speed. As a loose dough forms, add the egg and then the butter, bit by bit. Once it's one smooth ball, turn up the speed to medium-high and knead the dough until it's quite elastic and slapping at the sides of the bowl, about 10 minutes. Shape the dough into a ball and place it in a large, greased bowl. Cover with plastic wrap. Place in a warm space and let rise until doubled in size, about 3 hours, or in the fridge overnight. Congrats! You've made brioche dough.

**3.** Preheat the oven to 350°F. Dust your work surface with flour, and roll the dough out to a 16 by 10-inch rectangle with a thickness of ½ inch.

**4.** To fill and shape the rolls, spread the melted butter across the dough. Mix the sugar and cinnamon and sprinkle the mixture all over. Roll up the dough into a log, starting on the long side.

**5.** With a floured knife, slice the rolled-up dough crosswise into 1- to 2-inch slices. Each slice should look like a circle with a swirl in the middle. Grease a 10-inch round cast-iron skillet with butter. Lay in the slices of dough, swirl side up. Fill the entire pan with swirls. (If you want to save these until the morning, cover with plastic wrap and refrigerate; they'll be okay overnight.)

**6.** Bake for 25 to 30 minutes, until golden brown and puffed up. Pull the rolls out of the oven, and while still warm, cover with the glaze. Enjoy while still warm or cover with aluminum foil and gently reheat in the oven when you're ready to devour them.

# PIZZA, THREE WAYS

A **WOW** RECIPE

These recipes all use the same dough recipe
and all have the same rule: less is more. If you
pile on the sauce and cheese, you will get a
pooled depressing mess burned onto your
pizza stone. Just administer as much restraint
as possible and you'll be okay.

## henry's pizza dough

*For three 12- to 14-inch pizzas*

4½ cups bread flour, plus more for dusting
1½ tablespoons sugar
1 tablespoon kosher salt
2¼ teaspoons instant yeast (one ¼-ounce
   packet)
¼ cup extra virgin olive oil
2 cups warm water (about the temperature
   of bath water)

**1.** Combine the flour, sugar, salt, and yeast in
the bowl of a food processor. Pulse 3 or 4 times
until mixed. Add the olive oil and water. Run
the food processor until the dough forms a ball
that rides around the bowl above the blade,
about 15 seconds. Continue processing for 20
to 30 seconds longer. If you don't have a food
processor, a stand mixer with a dough hook is
fine. Just mix until the dough slaps the sides of
the bowl and gathers in a ball on the hook, 10 to
15 minutes.

**2.** Transfer the dough ball to a lightly floured
surface and knead once or twice by hand until
a smooth ball is formed. Tear off a golf ball–size
piece and stretch it with your hands. It should
easily stretch until you can sort of see light
through it. (This is known as the "windowpane

test.") Divide the dough into three equal parts
and place in three lightly oiled containers.
Cover with a lid or plastic wrap, and allow to
rise until doubled in size, 2 to 3 hours.

**3.** One hour before baking, adjust an oven rack
with a pizza stone to the middle position and
preheat the oven to 500°F. Turn a single dough
ball out onto a lightly floured surface. Gently
press out the dough into a rough 8-inch circle,
leaving the outer 1-inch edge thicker than the
rest. Gently stretch the dough, by draping it
over your knuckles, into a 12- to 14-inch circle,
about ¼-inch thick. Transfer to a pizza peel or
a rimless baking sheet. Top according to your
taste and bake as per the recipe directions.

## GOAT CHEESE PIZZA WITH CORN, RED ONION, AND PESTO

*For 3 pizzas*

**BASIL PESTO**
¾ cup fresh basil leaves, packed
¼ cup freshly grated Parmigiano
¼ cup pine nuts
2 medium garlic cloves, minced
⅓ cup extra virgin olive oil
Kosher salt and freshly ground black pepper

3 balls Henry's Pizza Dough (page 183)
¾ cup crumbled fresh goat cheese
Kernels cut from 2 ears corn
2 tablespoons extra virgin olive oil
¾ cup thinly sliced red onion

**1.** To prepare the pesto, combine the basil, Parmigiano, pine nuts, and garlic in a food processor and pulse to combine. Drizzle in the olive oil until a paste forms. Season with salt and pepper to taste. (You'll have more than you need for the 3 pizzas. Store the rest in a small container in the fridge for up to 2 weeks.

**2.** Spread about 3 tablespoons of the pesto onto a pizza. Top with ¼ cup of the goat cheese. Lightly coat the corn with about a tablespoon of the olive oil, then add one-third of the corn to the pizza along with ¼ cup of the onion. Sprinkle with salt and pepper.

**3.** Slide the pizza onto the baking stone and bake until the cheese is melted with some browned spots and the crust is golden brown and puffed, 12 to 15 minutes. Using a pizza peel or rimless baking sheet, lift the pizza out of the oven, transfer to a cutting board, slice, and serve immediately. Repeat with the remaining pizza dough and toppings.

## pizza sauce

*For 3 cups sauce*

2 tablespoons extra virgin olive oil
1 garlic clove, minced
½ teaspoon finely chopped fresh thyme
½ teaspoon finely chopped fresh rosemary
1 teaspoon finely chopped fresh oregano
¼ teaspoon chili flakes
1 cup finely chopped yellow onion
One 28-ounce can tomato puree
Kosher salt and freshly ground black pepper

In a saucepan over low heat, simmer together the olive oil, garlic, thyme, rosemary, oregano, and chili flakes for 5 minutes, or until the garlic is golden brown. Add the onion and turn the heat up to medium. Cook for an additional 5 minutes. The onion should be translucent and soft. Add the tomato puree and simmer for 15 minutes, until slightly thickened and the flavors have come together. Season with salt and pepper to taste. Store in a container in the fridge for up to 2 weeks.

## CLASSIC PEPPERONI PIZZA

*For 3 pizzas*

¾ cup Pizza Sauce (page 184)
3 balls Henry's Pizza Dough (page 183)
4 ounces fresh mozzarella, grated
⅓ pound finocchiona or pepperoni, thinly
   sliced
Kosher salt and freshly ground black pepper

1. Spread about ¼ cup of the sauce onto a pizza. Top with one-third of the mozzarella, then add one-third of the finocchiona or pepperoni. Sprinkle with salt and pepper.

2. Slide the pizza onto the baking stone and bake until the cheese is melted with some browned spots and the crust is golden brown and puffed, 12 to 15 minutes. Using a pizza peel or rimless baking sheet, lift the pizza out of the oven, transfer to a cutting board, slice, and serve immediately. Repeat with the remaining pizza dough, sauce, and toppings.

## PIZZA BIANCA

*For 3 pizzas*

1 large zucchini
Kosher salt
3 garlic cloves, minced
⅔ cup heavy cream
3 balls Henry's Pizza Dough (page 183)
1½ ounces fontina cheese, grated
1½ ounces mozzarella, grated
1½ ounces Parmigiano, grated
Freshly ground black pepper
Extra virgin olive oil

1. Halve the zucchini crosswise, then cut each half lengthwise into ⅛-inch-wide slices. Cut the slices lengthwise into ⅛-inch-thick strips. Toss with salt in a large medium-mesh sieve set over a bowl and drain for 30 minutes.

2. Squeeze handfuls of the zucchini to remove moisture, then roll up in a triple layer of paper towels and squeeze to remove any remaining moisture.

3. Combine the garlic and cream, then spread one-third of the mixture onto the pizza. Top with one-third of the fontina and mozzarella. Add one-third of the prepared zucchini and finish with one-third of the Parmigiano. Sprinkle with salt and pepper and drizzle with olive oil.

4. Slide the pizza onto the baking stone and bake until the cheeses are melted with some browned spots and the crust is golden brown and puffed, 12 to 15 minutes. Using a pizza peel or rimless baking sheet, lift the pizza out of the oven, transfer to a cutting board, slice, and serve immediately. Repeat with the remaining pizza dough and toppings.

# THE SWEET STUFF

No-Brainer Desserts and Decadent Treats

A good dessert makes up for a mediocre dinner. A good dessert can turn the tide of a bad date, and a dessert is the best cuddle buddy after a breakup. For me, I always want to eat dessert *now*, so I go one of two ways: simple and ready in no time, or make ahead and ready in my fridge anytime I want it. Whether it's Boy Bait Bread Pudding made with chocolate, stout, and brown butter (page 204), Blueberry Muffin Ice Cream with warm cinnamon streusel (page 207), or a Salted Caramel Pot de Crème with Bourbon Whipped Cream (page 203), dessert is *always* worth taking time to prepare, whether it's a meal that needs a little uplift or just your day.

# ALL ABOUT PIE

Whether it's the rich but simple Chocolate Pecan Derby Pie Bars, the bright and fresh No-Bake Strawberry–Lemon Verbena Pie, deliciously intricate Lemon Meringue Pie, or the showstopping Shaker Apple Pie scented with rose water, once you have the pie crust down, you can churn out any pie you'd like, all year long.

## PIE CRUST

This is a double-crust recipe. You can refrigerate the dough for 3 days or freeze for future use.

*For two 9-inch crusts*

2½ cups all-purpose flour
3 tablespoons sugar
1 teaspoon kosher salt
8 ounces (2 sticks) unsalted butter, cold, cut into small pieces
¼ to ½ cup ice water

1. In a food processor or quickly using your fingertips, combine the flour, sugar, salt, and butter until the chunks of butter are broken down to the size of peas and the flour feels like wet sand.

2. Add ¼ cup water and mix until the dough comes together easily. It's too dry if it immediately clumps apart. Add 2 tablespoons water at a time; you can always add more water but not more flour, so be careful not to add too much!

3. Gather the dough into two equal balls and plop them on top of two sheets of plastic wrap. Loosely wrap each ball and press down, smooshing the ball into a disk about 1-inch thick. Pop them into the fridge for at least 30 minutes while you busy yourself with the other stuff.

4. To prebake a pie crust: On a well-floured surface, roll out your dough to an 11-inch round, ⅛-inch thick, and place in the pie tin. Using a fork, prick the dough so it can release steam and won't bubble or warp. Place a sheet of parchment paper over the dough and fill with dried beans or pie weights. (This will prevent the dough from rising and will keep the sides from shrinking down.)

5. Bake it on the center rack at 425°F for 5 to 10 minutes or until the sides begin to brown. Remove the paper and beans and reduce the oven temperature to 375°F, baking for 5 more minutes or until golden brown. Cool completely.

## CHOCOLATE PECAN DERBY PIE BARS

A (YUM) RECIPE

Derby pie is part of the fabric that makes up the entire Derby Day. Almost like a combination of pecan pie, blondies, and brownies, derby pie is chocolatey and filled with golden brown sweetness and the tender crunch of pecans. It also couldn't be simpler to make. I amp mine up with a shortbread crust and a touch of bourbon, and serve it as bars for easy grabbing.

*For one 9 by 13-inch baking dish; about 24 bars, depending on how you slice*

### CRUST
2 cups all-purpose flour
8 ounces (2 sticks) unsalted butter, softened
½ cup powdered sugar
Pinch of kosher salt

### FILLING
4 large eggs
8 ounces (2 sticks) unsalted butter, melted
1 cup white sugar
1 cup light brown sugar, packed
1 tablespoon pure vanilla extract
2 tablespoons bourbon
1 cup all-purpose flour
1½ cups pecan halves, toasted
1½ cups chocolate chips

1. Preheat the oven to 350°F. Grease a 9 by 13-inch baking dish (I used a glass one). For easy removal, press a sheet of parchment paper into the greased dish, with edges going over the side of the dish. Grease the parchment. Once you're done baking, wait for the bars to cool and pull them out just by lifting the parchment up and out of the dish.

2. For the crust: Work together the flour, butter, powdered sugar, and salt until they form a dough. It should be moist but not sticky. Spread it on the bottom of the baking dish and pat down so it's evenly distributed. Bake for 20 to 25 minutes, until lightly golden brown. Set aside and get started on your filling, since you want the crust to still be quite hot when you pour filling on top.

3. For the filling: Beat together the eggs, butter, and white and brown sugars. Mix in the vanilla and bourbon. Add the flour a little at a time at low speed. With a wooden spoon or rubber spatula, fold in the pecans and chocolate chips and pour over the still hot crust.

4. Bake for 45 to 50 minutes, until the edges are firm and the center is set, not jiggly. Take out of the oven and cool completely before slicing. To store, cover with plastic wrap and keep on the counter for up to a week.

# NO-BAKE STRAWBERRY–LEMON VERBENA PIE

AN (MMM) RECIPE

Strawberries are wonderful at the peak of their season. Ripe, juicy, fragrant, sweet, and tender. My favorite part of the pie, though, is the lemon verbena whipped cream. It's the ultimate summer herb, imparting a citrus/mint/basil/earthy perfume to whatever it touches. Light, creamy, fresh, citrusy, and sweet, and all on a flakey butter pie crust, it's the dessert epitome of summer, and will be gone in a second.

*For one 9-inch pie*

⅔ cup white sugar
2½ tablespoons cornstarch
Pinch of kosher salt
1 quart fresh strawberries, quartered, plus more for garnish
1 teaspoon pure vanilla extract
2 tablespoons unsalted butter
2 tablespoons fresh lemon juice
1 teaspoon finely grated orange zest

## LEMON VERBENA WHIPPED CREAM
¼ cup white sugar
10 lemon verbena leaves (fresh or dried, and if they're hard to find, 4 segments of lemon peel are fine)
1½ cups heavy cream
1 teaspoon pure vanilla extract

½ Pie Crust recipe (page 188), or if you're short on time, store-bought, prebaked in a 9-inch pie tin.

1. For the filling, in a medium saucepan, combine the sugar, cornstarch, and salt. Blend in ⅔ cup water and 2½ cups of the strawberries. Bring to a boil, stirring and roughly smashing the strawberries. Boil, stirring constantly, until the mixture is very thick, a minute or so.

2. Remove from the heat and stir in the vanilla, butter, lemon juice, and orange zest. Cool to room temperature, then chill in the fridge.

3. For the lemon verbena whipped cream, combine the sugar with ¼ cup water in a small saucepan. Add the leaves. Simmer for 3 minutes, until the sugar is fully dissolved, and turn off the heat. Let the syrup cool completely. This can be done up to a week in advance for extra flavor.

4. Strain the syrup and add it to the cream along with the vanilla. Whip to soft peaks.

5. To finish the pie, pour the strawberry mixture into the pie crust. Top with the remaining fresh strawberries. Dollop the whipped cream in the center and spread, but reveal the strawberries at the edge. Garnish with sliced strawberries.

## TINA'S LEMON MERINGUE PIE

A (wow) RECIPE

Tina's pies are all so delicious that I polled my family on which to include. While the votes were tight, lemon meringue came out the winner and for good reason. Refreshing and tart but covered with heaps of soft, sweet meringue, it's a stunning pie and oh so delicious.

*For one 9-inch pie*

2 tablespoons grated lemon zest
½ cup fresh lemon juice (2 to 3 lemons)
4 large egg yolks (keep the whites for the
    meringue)
⅓ cup cornstarch
1½ cups white sugar
¼ teaspoon kosher salt
1¼ cups hot water
2 tablespoons unsalted butter, cut into
    pieces, softened

### MERINGUE
6 large egg whites (left from the filling
    with two added)
Pinch of kosher salt
¼ teaspoon cream of tartar
⅔ cup white sugar

½ recipe Pie Crust (page 188), or if you're
    short on time, store-bought, prebaked in
    a 9-inch pie tin

**1.** Place a rack in the center of the oven and preheat the oven to 375°F.

**2.** Mix the lemon zest and juice and set aside.

**3.** Place the egg yolks in a bowl, mix, and set aside.

**4.** Place the cornstarch, sugar, and salt in a heavy 2-quart saucepan and stir to mix. Gradually add the hot water, stirring with a rubber spatula until smooth. Place over medium heat and stir gently and constantly until the mixture comes to a low boil. Boil gently, stirring with the rubber spatula, for 5 minutes. Add the butter and stir briefly to melt. Remove from the heat.

**5.** Add a few large spoonfuls of the hot cornstarch mixture to the egg yolks and stir together. Pour the yolk mixture into the cornstarch mixture while continuing to stir. Mix in the lemon zest and juice. Return to medium heat and stir gently until the mixture comes to a boil again. Boil, stirring gently, for 5 minutes, or until quite thick (like the texture of loose pudding). Transfer the hot filling to a large bowl and let it cool completely, about an hour.

**6.** For the meringue, place the egg whites, salt, and cream of tartar in the bowl of a stand mixer. Beat at high speed with a whisk until the whites hold a soft point when the beaters are raised.

**7.** Reduce the speed to medium and gradually add the sugar, adding 2 tablespoons at a time and beating about 20 seconds between additions. Increase the speed to high again and beat only until the mixture holds a firm point when the beaters are raised—it should be stiff, but do not overbeat.

**8.** Pour the cooled lemon filling into the pie crust and top with the meringue. Make sure the meringue completely covers the filling and that it goes right up to the edge of the crust. Spread the meringue smooth all the way to the edge. With the back of a teaspoon, pull it up, forming peaks and swirls. (It is more attractive if the peaks are few and large rather than many and small.)

**9.** Bake for 8 to 10 minutes, until the meringue is golden. Have a draft-free spot (away from greedy neighborhood children) ready to cool the pie. (A draft could make the meringue fall or weep.) Place the pie on a wire rack and let it cool completely.

**10.** Chill completely in the fridge, at least 2 hours. The filling becomes firmer and easier to cut when refrigerated. Serve the pie the same day it's baked for best results.

## SHAKER APPLE PIE

AN (MMM) RECIPE

Rose water gives such a unique flavor to the apples, bringing out their fruitiness and ripened sweetness. For such a simple pie, you'll want to use the most flavorful apples you can find, such as Pink Lady, Granny Smith, Jonathan, or Braeburn, so that nothing masks that pure apple flavor.

*For one 9-inch double-crust pie*

8 cups peeled, cored, and sliced apples
   (⅜-inch thick)
¼ cup all-purpose flour
½ cup white sugar, plus more for
   sprinkling
½ cup light brown sugar, packed
1½ tablespoons heavy cream
¾ teaspoon rose water
1 recipe Pie Crust (page 188)

**EGG WASH**
½ teaspoon rose water
1 tablespoon heavy cream
1 large egg

1. Place a rack in the center of the oven and preheat the oven to 375°F.

2. Combine the apples, flour, sugars, cream, and rose water in a bowl, until everything is lightly coated.

3. To roll out the dough, let it sit at room temperature for 5 to 10 minutes. Sprinkle some flour on top of the dough as well as on your work surface. Roll out each piece to a 12-inch circle, about ⅛-inch thick. As you roll out the dough, use a metal spatula to check if the dough is sticking to your work surface. Add a few sprinkles of flour if necessary to keep the dough from sticking. Roll up one piece of dough onto the rolling pin, like a spool, and place on a 9-inch pie tin, lining up with the center of the pan. Gently unroll and press down to line the pie tin with the dough.

4. Fill with the apple slices, mounding a bit in the middle, and cover with the other layer of dough. Cut off the excess dough, leaving a 1-inch border around the tin. Pinch the edges to flute together (or press with a fork if that's easier), then cut three small vents into the top crust. Mix together the ingredients for the egg wash and brush over the top of the pie. Sprinkle with white sugar.

5. Bake for 50 to 60 minutes. If the edges brown too quickly, cover them with aluminum foil.

6. Let the apple pie cool until it's just warm, and the liquid has had time to settle.

## MOM'S PAVLOVA

A (WOW) RECIPE

My mom gave in to our every whim when it came to the birthday cake conversation: baked Alaska one year, a three-tiered wedding cake for my sister the next, but pavlova would always pop up around my birthday because it was the quintessential summer dessert. Light, sweet, and airy, just like the tutu of the ballerina it was named after.

---

### meringue
*For 1 large pavlova or 4 small*

½ cup superfine sugar
½ teaspoon cream of tartar
1 teaspoon cornstarch
2 large egg whites
Pinch of kosher salt
¼ teaspoon pure vanilla extract

**1.** Preheat the oven to 275°F.

**2.** Sift together the sugar, cream of tartar, and cornstarch. On low speed, mix the egg whites and salt for 1 to 2 minutes, until frothy. Go up to medium-high, gently adding in the dry ingredients. Once the meringue is glossy and forming soft peaks, anywhere from 4 to 10 minutes, depending on your mixer, finish on high speed and add the vanilla.

**3.** Spoon the meringue onto a baking sheet lined with a piece of parchment paper, and spread so it forms a layer ¼- to ½-inch thick (thicker for a larger pavlova), then add more meringue around the edge, forming a border of little peaks. It should be anywhere from 1 to 3 inches high, depending on how large your pavlova is.

**4.** Pop into the oven and bake for 50 to 60 minutes for small pavlovas, and 80 to 90 minutes for a large pavlova. It should be a slight beigey-pink and definitely *not* toasted.

**5.** Turn off the heat and crack the oven open. Let the pavlova cool to room temperature, then remove. (This is to prevent cracks and to cook it totally through.) You want it crisp on the outside and soft on the inside.

*Note: Fill the pavlova just before serving, since the whipping cream will dissolve the meringue over time. Combine the garnishing ingredients and sprinkle on top.*

## spring: fresh strawberries with rhubarb syrup

### WHIPPED CREAM
1 cup heavy cream
1 tablespoon white sugar
¼ teaspoon rose water
1 teaspoon pure vanilla extract
1 to 2 pints strawberries, halved or
    quartered

### SYRUP
1 cup quartered strawberries
1 cup sliced rhubarb, ¼-inch thick
2 tablespoons white sugar
1 tablespoon fresh lemon juice

1. For the whipped cream, whip together the cream, sugar, rose water, and vanilla until soft peaks form. Fold in the strawberries.

2. For the syrup, combine all the ingredients with ¼ cup water in a small pot over medium heat. Cook for about 15 minutes, until the syrup is deep red and coating the back of a spoon. Strain and cool completely.

3. To put the pavlova together, dollop with the strawberry whipped cream and drizzle with the syrup.

## summer: sliced peaches and blackberry sauce

### WHIPPED CREAM
1 cup heavy cream
1 tablespoon white sugar
1 teaspoon pure vanilla extract
2½ cups thinly sliced fresh peaches

### GARNISH
1 cup blackberries
1 tablespoon chopped fresh basil
1 tablespoon white sugar

1. For the whipped cream, whip together the cream, sugar, and vanilla until soft peaks form. Fold in the sliced peaches.

2. For the garnish, combine all the ingredients with ¼ cup water in a small pot over medium heat. Cook for about 15 minutes, until the blackberries are quite soft and the syrup is deep purple and coating the back of a spoon. Cool completely.

3. To put the pavlova together, dollop with the peach whipped cream and drizzle with the syrup.

## fall: vanilla poached pears

**WHIPPED CREAM**
1 cup heavy cream
1 tablespoon white sugar
1 teaspoon pure vanilla extract

**POACHED PEARS**
1 cup white sugar
¼ cup light brown sugar, packed
1 vanilla bean, split open and seeds
    scraped out and reserved
4 Bosc pears, peeled, quartered, and cored

1. For the whipped cream, whip together the cream, sugar, and vanilla until soft peaks form. Cover and refrigerate until needed.

2. For the poached pears, in a large saucepan, heat 4 cups water, the sugars, and vanilla bean and seeds and stir gently until the sugars are dissolved.

3. Cut a round of parchment paper the diameter of the saucepan and snip a small hole in the center. Slide the pears into the syrup and cover with the parchment paper. Keeping the liquid at a very low boil, simmer until the pears are cooked through, about 15 minutes.

4. Remove the pears from the liquid to cool. Turn the heat to high and simmer until the liquid is reduced to about a cup of syrup. (This will take 20 to 25 minutes.) Let cool.

5. To put the pavlova together, dollop with the whipped cream. Top with the pears and drizzle with the syrup.

## winter: mango citrus

1 cup heavy cream
1 tablespoon white sugar
1 teaspoon pure vanilla extract
1 orange
1 grapefruit
½ cup chopped fresh mango
2 tablespoons toasted coconut flakes

Whip together the cream, sugar, and vanilla until soft peaks form. Slice the skin off the orange and grapefruit and slice between the white membrane, segmenting the fruit. Fold the orange and grapefruit sections into the whipped cream, along with the mango. Dollop on top of the pavlova. Top with the toasted coconut.

## SALTED CARAMEL POT DE CRÈME WITH BOURBON WHIPPED CREAM

A **WOW** RECIPE

Pot de crème is French for pudding, more or less. French pudding is dense, rich, and luscious. Thickened with egg yolks and sweetened with homemade caramel sauce, these small cups of heaven are perfect to make the day before having people over.

*For six 4-ounce ramekins*

2 cups whole milk
1 vanilla bean, split open and seeds
    scraped out and reserved
1 large egg plus 1 egg yolk
1 tablespoon white sugar
1 cup Caramel Sauce (page 164)
Bourbon Whipped Cream (recipe follows)
About 1 teaspoon coarse sea salt, for
    garnish

**1.** Pour the milk in a small pot, and add the vanilla bean and seeds. Bring to barely a simmer, then turn off the heat. Cover and let infuse for 30 minutes.

**2.** Meanwhile, preheat the oven to 325°F.

**3.** In a bowl, beat the egg and egg yolk with the sugar, then slowly pour in the hot milk through a fine-mesh strainer. Discard the vanilla bean pod. Whisk together, then pour in ½ cup of the caramel and stir until dissolved.

**4.** Pour the remaining caramel into the bottoms of the ramekins. Remove any foam that might have formed on top of the crème mixture, then pour it into the ramekins. Place them in a baking dish, then pour hot water into the baking dish (careful not to get any in the ramekins!) so that the ramekins are half immersed.

**5.** Place in the middle of the oven and bake for 45 to 50 minutes. Check regularly after 30 minutes. The middle of the crèmes should jiggle a little; the crèmes will settle once they cool down.

**6.** Take the ramekins out and let them cool down. Place plastic wrap on top and place them in the fridge to rest for a few hours and completely chill before eating.

**7.** Serve topped with bourbon whipped cream and a little sea salt.

## bourbon whipped cream

½ cup heavy cream
1 tablespoon white sugar
1 teaspoon bourbon

Whip together the cream, sugar, and bourbon until soft peaks form.

# BOY BAIT BREAD PUDDING

AN (MMM) RECIPE

For this bread pudding I used brown butter and brown sugar to bring out the depth of the chocolate and highlight the maple/coffee notes that sometimes come through. Served with a dollop of whipped sour cream, this dessert is decadent but perfectly balanced, and even better the next day.

*For one 8-inch square baking dish or four 12-ounce ramekins*

2 tablespoons unsalted butter, plus more for the baking dish
1 baguette or French loaf (stale bread is perfect), cubed and dry (6 to 7 cups)
1 cup light brown sugar, packed
½ teaspoon fine sea salt
¼ cup unsweetened cocoa powder
3 cups half-and-half
3 teaspoons pure vanilla extract
6 tablespoons stout
6 large eggs, lightly beaten
8 ounces semisweet chocolate, grated or chopped
1 cup sour cream
2 tablespoons white sugar

**1.** Preheat the oven to 325°F.

**2.** Lightly grease an 8-inch square baking dish or four 12-ounce ramekins with butter and fill with the bread. Sift the brown sugar, salt, and cocoa into the half-and-half and mix well.

**3.** In another bowl, add 2 teaspoons of the vanilla and the stout to the beaten eggs.

**4.** To make the brown butter, melt the 2 table-spoons of butter over medium heat until the milk solids turn golden brown. Remove from the heat and pour into a bowl to cool. (It can still burn in the warm pan.) Combine with the eggs. Add to the cream mixture and mix well. Stir in the grated chocolate. Pour the mixture over the cubed bread in the baking dish. Let stand, stirring occasionally, for approximately 20 minutes, or until bread absorbs most of the liquid.

**5.** Set the baking dish in a larger baking pan. Fill the pan with water until it reaches an inch up the sides of the baking dish. Bake a large pudding for 1 hour and the small ramekins for 45 minutes, until set (it should be a little jiggly in the middle).

**6.** Remove from the oven and cool slightly. (You want to serve the pudding warm, not hot.)

**7.** Whip together the sour cream, white sugar, and the remaining teaspoon of vanilla until it forms soft peaks. Top the pudding with the whipped sour cream or serve on the side.

## BLUEBERRY MUFFIN ICE CREAM

A (WOW) RECIPE

Brown butter, vanilla, and brown sugar to give the base that "just baked" flavor, sweet-tart blueberry compote for that perfect swirl, and cinnamon streusel crumbled throughout for a bit of texture and that muffin-top taste. The brown butter ice cream is great by itself, but the blueberry muffin tweak is definitely worth a shot. You will need a candy thermometer for this recipe.

*For 1 quart ice cream*

8 tablespoons (1 stick) unsalted butter
3 cups half-and-half
3 large egg yolks
¼ cup white sugar
¼ cup light brown sugar, packed
¾ teaspoon kosher salt
2 teaspoons pure vanilla extract
¼ cup Blueberry-Lime Compote (page 208) or jam
3 tablespoons Cinnamon Streusel, plus more for garnish (page 208)
½ cup fresh blueberries

1. Melt the butter in a small pot over medium heat until it becomes golden brown. Remove from the heat and allow the butter to cool to room temperature.

2. In a large pot, bring the half-and-half to a simmer over medium heat.

3. Whisk together the egg yolks, sugars, and salt until smooth. To temper the eggs, carefully whisk about 1 cup of the hot half-and-half into the egg mixture until smooth. Then whisk the egg mixture back into the half-and-half in the pot. Return to medium-low heat and cook to 170°F, constantly stirring along the bottom of the pot to ensure even cooking. Once it has reached 170°F, remove from the heat and whisk in the vanilla and brown butter. Strain through a fine-mesh strainer into a bowl. Cool the ice cream base, in its bowl, to room temperature in an ice bath, then pop the base into the fridge to fully chill, at least 2 hours.

4. Once the base is chilled, process it in your ice cream maker. When it's somewhere between soft serve and ice cream from the freezer, transfer the ice cream to a large bowl, fold in the blueberry compote, then the streusel, so it ribbons through the ice cream. Put in a container and freeze until firm. Garnish with fresh blueberries when serving.

*(continued on page 208)*

## blueberry-lime compote

*For 1 pint*

4 half-pints blueberries
Juice of 3 limes
1 cup white sugar

Clean 1-pint jar. Combine everything in a bowl, then heat in a medium pot over medium heat until the blueberries liquefy and when you stir a spoon through it, you can see the bottom of the pan for a beat. (Basically, it should look kind of syrupy.) Pour into the jar, tighten the lid, flip upside down, and let cool until room temperature. Keep refrigerated for at least 6 hours, and then use whenever you like.

## cinnamon streusel

*For ¾ cup*

½ cup all-purpose flour
¼ cup white sugar
Pinch of kosher salt
1 teaspoon ground cinnamon
2 ounces cold unsalted butter, cubed

1. Using your fingers or a food processor, combine the flour, sugar, salt, and cinnamon. Mix in the butter until crumbly. Place on a baking sheet lined with a silicone mat and bake at 350°F for 10 minutes. Break apart and mix up the streusel.

2. Bake for another 10 minutes or until golden brown. Crumble and cool.

## DARK CHOCOLATE SORBET

A YUM RECIPE

If you're a dark chocolate purist, sorbet is where it's at. It's basically chocolate, but frozen. I like to add a little bit of coffee and brown sugar to really bring out the rich dark chocolate flavor. This is a recipe that lives or dies on the quality of the ingredients, so make sure to use the best cocoa powder and dark chocolate you can find. (I used Valrhona, a French chocolate company.)

*For 1 quart sorbet*

6 ounces bittersweet chocolate, roughly chopped
¾ cup unsweetened cocoa powder (not Dutch processed)
½ cup white sugar
¼ cup light brown sugar, packed
1½ teaspoons pure vanilla extract
¼ cup brewed coffee
¼ teaspoon kosher salt

1. Melt the chocolate in a heatproof bowl over a pot of boiling water or in the top of a double boiler. Make sure the water isn't touching the bowl. Add the rest of the ingredients and 2 cups water and stir until the mixture has a smooth, shiny consistency. Remove from the heat.

2. Cover with plastic wrap and chill in the fridge overnight.

3. Process the sorbet in your ice cream maker, as per the manufacturer's guide, or until it has the consistency of soft serve (15 to 20 minutes, depending on the machine). Transfer to a container. Pop the lid on and freeze for at least 2 hours to set before serving.

# BROWN BETTY ICE CREAM

AN (MMM) RECIPE

One of my favorite ice cream discoveries was switching out white sugar for brown sugar. All of a sudden boring old vanilla is transformed into an edgier, richer version of itself. I add brown butter and bourbon to this combination to really push it over the top.

*For 2 pints ice cream*

4 ounces (1 stick) unsalted butter
3 cups half-and-half
3 large egg yolks
½ cup light brown sugar, packed
¾ teaspoon kosher salt
2 teaspoons pure vanilla extract
1 ounce (2 tablespoons) bourbon

**1.** Simmer the butter over medium heat until it takes on a nice golden-brown color. Remove from the heat and allow to cool to room temperature.

**2.** In a large pot, bring the half-and-half almost to a boil over medium-high heat. Meanwhile, whisk together the yolks, sugar, and salt until smooth. To temper the egg mixture, carefully whisk about 1 cup of the hot cream into the eggs until smooth. Then whisk the egg mixture back into the remaining cream in the pot. Return to medium-low heat, and cook up to 170°F, constantly stirring along the bottom of the pot to ensure even cooking. Once it has reached 170°F, remove from the heat and whisk in the vanilla, bourbon, and brown butter.

**3.** Strain through a wire-mesh strainer into a heatproof bowl. Cool down to room temperature in an ice bath. Pop into the fridge to fully chill (at least 2 hours).

**4.** Once the mixture is chilled through, put it in your ice cream maker. Once it's gotten firm, put in a container and freeze until firmed up completely.

## SALTED HONEY PEANUT BUTTER ICE CREAM

AN  RECIPE

Topped with a fresh caramel sauce, this treat evangelizes the peanut butter nonbelievers, myself included. I can't put down this sweet-salty-nutty dessert, so if you actually like peanut butter, this is a must-try.

*For 2 pints ice cream*

3 cups half-and-half
¾ cup light brown sugar, packed
2 large egg yolks
¾ cup honey-roasted peanut butter (If you
   only have regular, add 2 tablespoons of
   honey.)
¾ teaspoon coarse sea salt, plus more to
   taste
2 tablespoons honey
1 teaspoon pure vanilla extract
Caramel Sauce (page 164), for serving
   (optional)
Roasted peanuts, for serving (optional)

**1.** In a medium pot over low heat, bring the half-and-half to a simmer. Add the sugar and stir to dissolve.

**2.** In a bowl, whisk the egg yolks. Add a little of the hot half-and-half and whisk to combine. Add a little more, then pour the contents of the bowl into the pan and stir until thickened, or until the temperature reaches 170°F.

**3.** Off the heat, add the peanut butter, sea salt, honey, and vanilla, stirring to combine. Chill in the fridge for at least 2 hours.

**4.** Process in your ice cream maker and freeze as recommended.

**5.** To serve, scoop out and, if you like, drizzle with caramel sauce and sprinkle with sea salt and roasted peanuts.

# MAGIC CHINESE EGG PUFFS

AN (MMM) RECIPE

I had egg puffs for the first time at a Chinese dumpling house in San Francisco. A waiter walked by with a tray of puffy, golden-brown clouds and I knew I had to have them. Pulling one apart with both hands revealed a custardy center and beautifully crisp exterior. Not too sweet and oh so tender, I had to have these again, and I promised myself it would be in my own kitchen. The trick is to whisk the dough until your arms are sore to get it smooth, and be careful not to add too many to the oil since they puff up like mad.

*For 16 egg puffs*

Canola oil, for deep-frying
2 tablespoons unsalted butter
1 tablespoon white sugar, plus ¼ cup for
    coating
¼ teaspoon kosher salt
1¼ cups all-purpose flour
4 large eggs, beaten

**1.** Pour the oil into a 5-quart Dutch oven or heavy-bottomed pot about 1½ inches deep. Heat the oil over medium-high heat until it reaches 350°F. If the oil is ready before the batter, lower the heat to keep the oil hot.

**2.** Meanwhile, in a medium pot over medium heat, heat the butter, 1 cup water, the 1 tablespoon sugar, and the salt until the butter has melted and the water begins to bubble at the side of the pot. Remove the pot from the heat and add the flour right away. Stir vigorously with a whisk until well blended. You'll need some upper-body strength for this, so I recommend using an electric mixer to make this part easier. Place the pot back on the burner (don't turn on the heat), and continue to stir until a ball of dough comes together and doesn't stick to the side of the pot.

**3.** Transfer the dough to a medium bowl. If the dough is still hot, stir it for 15 to 30 seconds to cool it. Pour in one-quarter of the eggs and stir until all of the egg has been absorbed. (It won't look like it's mixing in at first, but keep at it.) Continue until all the eggs have been mixed into the dough and the dough is thick and smooth.

**4.** Use two spoons to scoop up about 2 tablespoons of batter and push it into the oil. You should have 8 puffs frying for each of two batches. Fry for 8 to 10 minutes, turning frequently, until the puffs have puffed up significantly (about three times their original size). They are done when they are light golden brown on each side. Return the oil to 350°F before frying the second batch.

**5.** Drain the puffs for a few minutes on a paper towel and coat with sugar. Serve warm. The puffs stay tasty for about an hour after frying.

# ENTERTAINING IN A SNAP

How to Cook, Host, and Still Have Fun

The prospect of a room full of people you're supposed to feed, give drinks to, and entertain sends most of us (including me) running for cover. In truth, I'm an introvert. I love cooking and planning, but the idea of maintaining the interest of a group of people terrifies me. I'm the corner talker, that person who has a deep and long-winded discussion with a stranger in the corner of the room, only emerging for air to go to the ladies' or to leave at 11:30 so I can get to sleep by 12. But recently, I realized that I could be a gardener as opposed to a puppet master. I just plant my seeds for fun and watch them grow: good music, good drinks, good people, and an activity or theme to gather everyone's attention and anchor the evening.

# HOW TO BE THE HOST WHILE MAINTAINING YOUR SANITY

First off, a disclaimer: If you are inviting people over, you are "hosting" them. There is no escaping this fact, so let's just take a deep breath and get over the pressure and expectations we associate with having guests. Here are some of the dos and don'ts that I've learned.

**1. Make a playlist.** Music fills in awkward pauses in conversation and sets the tone for the evening. Once you make a great party playlist, you never have to make it again. Choose songs with an upbeat energy and mix in a few instrumentals so people can hear each other talk.

**2. Make it mostly BYOB.** You're inviting your friends, right? Your home is not a bar, so why should you be expected to provide unlimited booze for the evening? Have enough for 1 or 2 drinks per person: a few bottles of your favorite wine or the mix for your favorite cocktail on hand, but beyond that, feel free to delegate to your friends.

**3. When someone offers to help, accept!** I cannot tell you how many times I've insisted, "No, I'm fine" when the answer should've been, "Great! Can you come over early and help me set up?" or "Can you stay late and help me clean dishes?"

**4. In fact, invite a couple of your closest friends to come over and help you set up, drink wine, get dressed, light candles, etc.** You will feel so much better when the doorbell rings and you're not alone in your apartment with someone's kind of awkward plus one, waiting for everyone else to arrive.

**5. Set a definitive start and end time.** If you send out an invitation that says 8:00 p.m. to 3:00 a.m., people are going to start showing up at 11:00 p.m. If you say 8 to 11, people are ringing the doorbell at 8:45. Decide what kind of party you want, and plan accordingly. A big bash will run a little later (10 to 2), and an easy-going cocktail party will run a little earlier (8 to 12). Any earlier than eight o'clock and people will probably expect food, since you're cutting into their dinnertime.

**6. Flattering lighting is key.** If you don't have dimmers, keep most of your lights off and light some candles, or buy lower-wattage bulbs. You want your space to feel cozy and warm. No one looks good under bright incandescent light, and you don't need the wrath of a friend who stumbled into bad lighting while attempting to flirt to dampen your night.

**7. Keep it simple.** You're having people over and you want to impress them, but now is not the time to experiment. It's the time to be happily relaxed while dazzling your friends with your wit and charm. The trick is to choose two or three dishes you're comfortable with, and make sure one of them is an "assembly only" platter such as a cheese board, crudités, an assortment of nuts, olives, or whatever you like. It's always better to have a few delicious crowd-pleasers than a table of "meh." And anyway, for those last ten minutes before the party starts, you'll want to be putting finishing touches on yourself, not the food.

**8. Organize an activity.** It doesn't have to be charades, but find something to anchor the evening and encourage your guests to interact. It can be the theme or reason for the party (a birthday, holiday, or season premiere of your favorite show); a fun game like Apples to Apples; or even a blind tasting where everyone brings a bottle of wine, you cover up the labels, everyone debates which one's the best, and the winner gets sent home with a goofy prize. By giving the extroverts a forum to show off their charisma and the wallflowers the opportunity to feel included, everyone will end up having a good time, including yourself.

**9. Be polite.** This sounds obvious, but sometimes our efforts at cutting corners can get the best of us at the expense of our guests' enjoyment. Example: My sister went to an early evening cocktail party at a friend's house, stomach grumbling because she was told there would be snacks. Looking around a wasteland of red plastic cups, she didn't see any food. "Where is it?" she wondered. "Oh, in the freezer. I figured if anyone was hungry, they could just heat something up," chimed the hostess. *Right.* No guest wants to rustle around your kitchen in the midst of a party to heat up some freeze-dried goodies. I'm sure this was an honest mistake, and the food was more of an afterthought than anything, but if the hostess didn't want to bother serving food, she could have started the party an hour later, or had a friend bring snacks. My point here is to be aware of your guests' needs. If you're not up for it, make a reservation at a nice restaurant or bar instead, or scale the event down to just a couple of your friends and a bottle of wine. No shame in that!

**10. Communicate.** This is the golden rule of hosting, the theme tying all of the previous tips together. Another way of putting it is "Manage your expectations." You can't expect people to

know something they haven't been told or to be aware of a boundary that hasn't been drawn. When it comes to the guest list, drinks, food (is anyone a vegetarian?), house rules (is it a no-shoes-indoors home?), make sure everyone's aware ahead of time. As I said before, you want to create an atmosphere where people can have fun and relax, and if everyone's aware of what's up, there won't be any unexpected blunders.

# PARTY MENUS

## GIRLS' MOVIE NIGHT

Bourbon Milk Shakes (page 258)
Lemon Truffle Caprese Pops (page 233)
Honey-Truffle Grilled Cheese (page 256)
Pizza Bianca (page 185)
Chocolate Sablé Caramel Bites (page 164)

## LADIES' BRUNCH

Black Rosemary Fizz (page 259)
Asparagus–White Corn Quiche (page 37)
Cherry Tomato Upside-Down Tart (page 26)
Rosemary, Potato, and Kale Tart (page 24)
Mesclun Greens with Avocado and Homemade
　　Pita Chips (page 110)
French Breakfast Puffs (page 170)

## BOYS' BRUNCH

Bloody Mary Bar (page 260)
Baked Eggs, American-style (page 38)
Pig Candy (page 241)
Blackberry Jam and Cream Cheese–Stuffed
　　Pain Perdu (page 19)

## DATE NIGHT

Classic Old-Fashioned (page 262)
Kale Salad with Gremolata Breadcrumbs,
　　Parmigiano, and Mustard and Lemon
　　Vinaigrette (page 99)
Perfect Steak (page 138)
Roasted Vegetables with Chimichurri (page 112)
Salted Caramel Pot de Crème with Bourbon
　　Whipped Cream (page 203)

## BEACH PICNIC

Toasted Coconut Vanilla Limeade (page 263)
The Perfect Avocado Sandwich with Garlic Aïoli
　　(page 121)
Israeli Couscous with Sautéed Mushrooms and
　　Goat Cheese (page 104)
Root Beer–Marinated Skirt Steak Sandwich
　　(page 137)
Blue Ribbon Cookies (page 168)

## BEER TASTING

Beer Fashioned (page 264)
Grilled Cheese with Apple Jelly, Cinnamon, and
　　Cheddar (page 257)
Cheese board (page 245)
Pig Candy (page 241)
Citrus-Marinated Olives (page 238)
Boy Bait Bread Pudding (page 204)

## TACO NIGHT

Spicy Roasted Pineapple Lemon-Limeade with
　　Tequila (page 267)
Tacos, Por Favor (page 156)
　　Camarones al Diablo (page 156)
　　Carne Asada with Sriracha Glaze (page 158)
　　Adobo-Scented Grilled Chicken (page 158)
　　Cola Carnitas (page 159)
Trio of Salsas (page 242)
Mexican Street Corn (page 117)
Pineapple Chili Pops (page 238)

## SUMMER DINNER PARTY

Sangria Blanca (page 266)
Goat Cheese, Arugula, and Nectarine Crostini
 (page 253)
Spicy Steak Salad (page 103)
Fresh Mozzarella with Summer Plums and Wal-
 nuts (page 249)
Quinoa Panzanella Salad (page 97)
S'meaches (page 235)

## DERBY DAY PARTY

Whitney's Rose Water Mint Julep (page 265)
Cheddar-Chive Grits Cakes with Cola Carnitas
 (page 237)
Coconut-Sriracha Fried Chicken (page 141)
Fuji Apple Salad with Bacon, Arugula, and
 Maple-Yogurt Dressing (page 96)
Chocolate Pecan Derby Pie Bars (page 191)

## BACKYARD BBQ

Spicy Yellow Nectarine Agua Fresca (page 268)
Henry's Burger (page 134)
Spring Potato Salad with Peas, Mint, and Eggs
 (page 107)
Grilled Corn Salad with Feta and Bacon (page 105)
Summer Pavlova: Sliced Peaches and Black-
 berry Sauce (page 200)

# THE HOSTESS HOW-TO'S

You can go crazy preparing a dinner for four close friends and be completely laid-back about a bbq for twenty. It all depends on approach, delegation, and priorities. Basically, get ready to be the commander of your kitchen. As with my recipes, I break the hostess how-to's down into three categories: Yum, Mmm, and Wow.

## A YUM PARTY

This is for those novice hosts among us. The easiest way to throw a simple get-together? Make it about something.

- Beer Tasting (see below)
- Girls' Movie Night (see page 220 for menu)
- Sunday TV catch-up night

These are events where you're inviting friends you love, friends who know you, and maybe a few on the periphery who you want to invite into the pack. The tone is casual, so the expectations aren't super high. You're looking at snacks, some drinks, and maybe dessert.

## SAMPLE PLAN: BEER TASTING

This is all about relaxing, so make your guests comfortable! Have them over at 8:00 p.m. and tell each to bring their favorite beer. Plan on a couple of easily assembled dishes, and enlist a friend to help with flipping grilled cheese and mixing Beer Fashioneds. Pick out some of your favorite low-key tunes (think your "study mix" from when you had finals) and dim the lights a little. When your friends arrive, serve the drinks with pig candy and a cheese board. Set up the beers from lightest to heaviest, and get to tasting!

## menu

Beer Fashioned (page 264)
Grilled Cheese with Apple Jelly, Cinnamon, and
    Cheddar (page 257)
Cheese board (page 245)
Pig Candy (page 241)
Citrus-Marinated Olives (page 238)
Boy Bait Bread Pudding (page 204)

## guest list

8 to 10 of your favorite beer nerds

## invitation

E-mail

## setup

Music
Ice buckets for beers
Tumblers for Beer Fashioneds

## helpers

1 friend to help with grilled cheese and cocktails

## AN (MMM) PARTY

You're comfortable with people coming over, you're happy to have a friend or two help, and you want to take it to the next level. This means a little more planning. You're throwing an actual party, so that means more guests, more food, more everything.

• Summer Dinner Party (see below)
• Boys' Brunch (see page 220 for menu)

## SAMPLE PLAN: SUMMER DINNER PARTY

This is still a pretty casual affair, but it's a little more "full on." You're serving a complete meal with appetizers and a cocktail, plus open flames! The trick here is in the planning: what to make ahead, when to set up, who does what, and all that other fun stuff. The day before, do your big shop. Leave everything out that doesn't need to be in the fridge, place all of your votives or lights, and organize your serving ware and set aside. Then make the quinoa salad.

The morning of, have your friend handle the sangria while you make the steak salad, mozzarella platter, and prep the crostini. Two hours before, organize the S'meaches tray and put together the crostini. An hour before, put any beers on ice if you're serving them. Thirty minutes before, have your friend set up the plates and cutlery, and light all the candles. Turn on your favorite lighthearted music.

Let the guests settle in with Sangria Blanca and the crostini. After everyone's arrived, get them seated. After dinner, hand out skewers and have guests toast marshmallows and peaches for their dessert.

## menu

Sangria Blanca (page 266)
Goat Cheese, Arugula, and Nectarine Crostini (page 253)
Spicy Steak Salad (page 103)
Fresh Mozzarella with Summer Plums and Walnuts (page 249)
Quinoa Panzanella Salad (page 97)
S'meaches (page 235)

## guest list

8 to 12

## invitation

E-mail or snail mail

## setup

Music
Grill
Outdoor space blankets
Skewers (for S'meaches)
Pitchers (for sangria cocktails)
Votive candles or string lights

## helpers

1 friend for the grill, cocktails, and setup
Second friend to help with clean-up

You're finally doing it. Pulling out the big guns. An epic meal, delicious cocktails, and some serious charm are in store for your guests. Intimidating? Yes, but that doesn't mean you shouldn't go for it! The difference here is the extent of actual "hosting." That means focusing on the details: the decor, the invitations, the spread, all of the lovely little things that elevate a casual get-together to a formal shindig.

Some perfect opportunities to flex your hostess muscles:

- Derby Day Party
- Ladies' Brunch (wedding and baby showers, for instance)
- New Year's Eve

## SAMPLE PLAN: DERBY DAY PARTY

The day before, do all of your shopping, make the rose water syrup for the juleps, measure out ingredients for the derby bars, and make the grits cakes up to the point before you bake them. Make the carnitas and the salad dressing and marinate the chicken. Bake the derby pie bars and let them cool.

The morning of the party, have your friend put together the apple salad, undressed; keep it in the fridge until ready to serve. Set up the tables with vintage tablecloths and put together a few bouquets of roses for each table.

Fry the chicken, bake it off in the oven, and set aside. Two hours before, bake the grits cakes. Heat up the carnitas and, if needed, the fried chicken, too.

An hour before, start assembling the mint julep station; cut up the derby pie bars and plate

them; and set up the salad with the dressing in a pitcher on the side.

Thirty minutes before, finish assembling the grits cakes and lay out the rest of the food. Turn on your favorite laid-back music. This party is all about fun drinks and fun conversation, so pick music that doesn't overpower the room or the race on the TV. Let the guests settle in with their mint juleps, big hats, and seersucker. Direct everyone to the buffet and have a fabulous time!

## menu

Whitney's Rose Water Mint Juleps (page 265)
Cheddar-Chive Grits Cakes with Cola Carnitas (page 237)
Coconut-Sriracha Fried Chicken (page 141)
Fuji Apple Salad with Bacon, Arugula, and Maple-Yogurt Dressing (page 96)
Chocolate Pecan Derby Pie Bars (page 191)

## guest list

15 to 20

## invitation

Snail mail

## setup

Vintage tablecloths

Large hats

Seersucker

Mint julep cups

Red roses

TV for watching the race

Printouts of the horses' names for friendly
betting

Prizes for winner of the betting pool (May I
suggest a bottle of bourbon?)

## helpers

1 friend for mixing mint juleps

Second friend for decor setup and clean-up

Third friend to help with serving the food, organizing bets

# PARTY RECIPES

## PROSCIUTTO-WRAPPED PEACH WITH MINT AND SERRANO CHILE

A **YUM** RECIPE

Prosciutto with fruit is a classic combination. Pairing earthy, melt-in-your-mouth dry-cured ham with the sweetness and acid of ripe fruit is a dynamite combination and the perfect no-brainer appetizer. This quick little app is one of my favorite summer bites, especially when yellow peaches are at their peak. The freshness of the mint and heat from the chile add an unexpected kick.

*For 8 pieces*

1 yellow peach
4 thin slices prosciutto, halved crosswise
8 fresh mint leaves
1 serrano chile, thinly sliced

Cut the peach into 8 slices and wrap each with a piece of prosciutto. Press 1 mint leaf onto each wrapped peach slice, and press a slice of serrano chile on top.

## LEMON TRUFFLE CAPRESE POPS

A **YUM** RECIPE

Sweet and mild mozzarella with the caramel-ized flavor of roasted tomatoes, combined with bright lemon zest, the herbaceous zing of basil, and that earthy, deep punch that truffle salt adds to anything make these a wallop of an hors d'oeuvre. There's barely any actual cooking, so line up a girlfriend or two and get a pre-party assembly line going.

*For 24 skewers*

24 cherry tomatoes
Kosher salt and freshly ground black pepper
Extra virgin olive oil
24 mini mozzarella balls (aka ciliegine),
    or fresh mozzarella cut into bite-size
    pieces (about 1 inch)
24 fresh basil leaves
1 tablespoon grated lemon zest
1 teaspoon truffle salt or truffle oil

**1.** Heat the oven to 425°F. Line a baking sheet with parchment paper.

**2.** Place the cherry tomatoes on the baking sheet and sprinkle with salt, pepper, and olive oil. Roast for about 20 minutes, until the toma-toes are wrinkled and their bottoms are cara-melized. Set aside to cool.

**3.** Pop a mozzarella ball onto a skewer, leaving about 1 inch of the skewer below. Roll a piece of basil up like a scroll and pierce it through the middle on top of the mozzarella. Add a cherry tomato on top. Repeat until you've done them all, then arrange the pops on a platter. Sprinkle with lemon zest and truffle salt. Finish with a drizzle of olive oil.

## SPICY ROASTED CHICKPEAS

AN  RECIPE

Bar snacks tend to be on the salty, spicy side, perfectly whetting your thirst for a refreshing drink. These chickpeas are no different, and are one of my favorite savory snacks to nosh on in between beers. Crunchy and just barely spicy, you'll be eating these by the handful.

*For 2 cups chickpeas*

Two 15.5-ounce cans chickpeas
¼ cup extra virgin olive oil
1½ teaspoons kosher salt, plus more for
    garnish
Moroccan Spice (page 113)

1. Preheat the oven to 400°F. Line a rimmed baking sheet with paper towels.

2. Drain and rinse the chickpeas and scatter on the baking sheet. Let stand, draining on the paper towels, for 15 minutes. (The drier they are, the crunchier they'll be.)

3. Remove the towels and toss the chickpeas with the olive oil, salt, and Moroccan Spice. Roast until crisp and golden, 45 minutes to 1 hour, stirring occasionally. They should be a very dark golden brown with crisp edges.

4. Toss with additional salt and serve.

## S'MEACHES

A **YUM** RECIPE

To add to something as perfect as a ripe summer peach seems like sacrilege, but the burnt sugar with a hint of spice and the sweet marshmallow against the acid of the fruit all work somehow. This is my new campfire favorite.

*For 8 S'meaches*

¼ teaspoon cayenne pepper
½ cup light brown sugar
1 peach, cut into 8 slices and halved
    horizontally
8 marshmallows
8 double graham crackers

**1.** Combine the cayenne and sugar, and toss in the peaches, mixing to coat.

**2.** Put 1 peach slice and 1 marshmallow on each of 8 skewers. Use metal skewers or soak wooden skewers in water 30 minues before using.

**3.** Toast over a medium-low flame until caramelized and browned.

**4.** Lay a peach-marshmallow skewer on a graham cracker half. Pull out the skewer. Sandwich with another graham cracker. Enjoy immediately!

## CHEDDAR-CHIVE GRITS CAKES WITH COLA CARNITAS

A **WOW** RECIPE

A combination of two recipes, these little guys are as close to a "fancy" hors d'oeuvre as I get. A tasty combination of rich, savory meat and creamy baked grits, these bites are great with a touch of sour cream and chives.

*For 24 grits cakes*

### GRITS CAKES
1 recipe Cheddar-Chive Grits (page 29), freshly cooked
Kosher salt and freshly ground black pepper
5 tablespoons chopped chives
½ recipe Cola Carnitas (page 159), warmed
½ cup sour cream

1. Season the grits with salt, pepper, and 1 tablespoon of the chives, and spread into a 9 by 13-inch baking dish in one layer about ¼- to ½-inch thick. Allow to cool completely.

2. Preheat the oven to 350°F.

3. Once the grits have set, take a 2-inch cookie cutter and cut out rounds. Place the rounds on a baking sheet lined with parchment paper. Roll the remaining grits together with your hands, then pat down to ¼- to ½-inch thick. Cut out more rounds and repeat this until you're out of grits. Bake for 10 to 15 minutes, until the grits cakes are golden brown at the edges.

4. Top the grits cakes with the carnitas and garnish with the sour cream and remaining chives. Serve while warm.

## CITRUS-MARINATED OLIVES

A YUM RECIPE

This is a briny, salty snack, perfect for guests to nibble on while you get the main course ready. Make sure to serve with plenty of toothpicks and a bowl for discarding pits.

*For 2 cups olives*

2 cups brined olives
1 lemon, thinly sliced into rounds
½ orange, thinly sliced into rounds
1 tablespoon finely chopped fresh cilantro
1 tablespoon finely chopped fresh flat-leaf
  parsley
2 garlic cloves, thinly sliced
½ red onion, thinly sliced
Extra virgin olive oil, for garnish

1. Combine all the ingredients except the olive oil and let them mingle together in the fridge for at least an hour.

2. Pour into a bowl and drizzle with olive oil. Serve with cocktails or a cheese board!

## PINEAPPLE CHILI POPS

A YUM RECIPE

There should be a "non-recipe" chapter to this book, because I love things that come together with little preparation. Especially when hors d'oeuvres can be so complicated and time-consuming, it's nice to have a no-brainer that guests will love to add to the mix.

*For 5 cups pineapple*

2 teaspoons ancho chile powder
½ teaspoon chili powder
½ teaspoon chipotle chile powder
½ teaspoon coarse sea salt
1 whole ripe pineapple

1. Combine the spices and salt.

2. Slice the skin off the pineapple and cut into fourths from top to bottom. Remove the fibrous core from each wedge, then chop the pineapple into large bite-size chunks.

3. Pop the pineapple onto toothpicks and sprinkle with the chili salt. Serve immediately.

# PIG CANDY

A **YUM** RECIPE

This is an old favorite that I make *every* time I have people over. It's just one of those slam-dunk bites that everyone loves. Smoky, salty, spicy, sweet, and ridiculously easy to make. In 30 minutes you'll have a bowl of kitsch bar snacks that are just as delicious with a rich red wine as with a spicy ale or sweet and smoky stout. The possibilities are endless and so is my appetite for these little pieces of heaven. In the words of the ad man, bet you can't eat just one.

*For 4 servings*

1 cup light brown sugar, packed
½ teaspoon cayenne pepper
8 slices thin-cut bacon

**1.** Preheat the oven to 350°F.

**2.** Meanwhile, blend the sugar and cayenne together in a bowl. Taste it. If it's too spicy, add more sugar; not spicy enough, add more cayenne. However, the spice does become a little more pronounced after being cooked, so keep that in mind.

**3.** Lay the bacon on a wire rack in a rimmed baking sheet lined with aluminum foil (this means minimal clean-up!). Cover each slice of bacon with the brown sugar mixture. It should be an even layer, thick enough that you cannot see the bacon through it (⅛- to ¼-inch). Bake for about 15 minutes, until the sugar is completely browned and the bacon has curled at the edges and appears mostly cooked.

**4.** Remove the bacon from the oven and flip. Cover the bacon with the rest of the brown sugar mixture and pop back into the oven for another 5 to 10 minutes, or until the bacon is cooked how you like it. If the bacon seems underdone, just leave it in the oven for a minute or two more.

**5.** Let the bacon cool on the rack for at least 15 minutes to let the sugar harden a bit before you start cutting the pieces. I find it's easiest to use a pair of kitchen scissors and cut the pieces over the serving bowl. Serve it up with the libation of your choice!

# TRIO OF SALSAS

A (YUM) RECIPE

It's always useful to have a few salsa recipes up your sleeve. They're simple to make and you can perfect them exactly to your taste. They're also a fantastic treat to bring to a daytime party when a bottle of wine feels too stuffy. Just make sure you bring enough tortilla chips!

## red salsa

*For about 3 cups salsa*

8 garlic cloves
½ red onion, roughly chopped
½ bunch fresh cilantro, leaves roughly
chopped
One 28-ounce can whole tomatoes
One 12-ounce can whole tomatillos
1 teaspoon ground cumin
2 tablespoons whole-grain Dijon mustard
1 tablespoon hot sauce
Juice of ½ lemon
1 tablespoon Worcestershire sauce
¼ cup pale ale
Kosher salt

**1.** Place the garlic, onion, and cilantro into a food processor. Blitz for a few seconds.

**2.** Add the liquid from the can of tomatoes, 4 tomatoes, 4 tomatillos, and ¼ cup of the tomatillo pickling liquid. (Save the leftover tomatoes and tomatillos in the fridge for future use.) Add everything else. Blend the whole thing. It should be on the liquid side rather than on the thick side. Personally, I like salsa that is either near liquid or in complete chunks. Not that weird marinara-esque in-between.

**3.** Season with salt to taste and there you go: a super simple, easy salsa that will keep them coming back for more. It's even better after sitting in the fridge or on the counter for a few hours.

## smoky salsa

*For 4 cups salsa*

One 28-ounce can whole tomatoes
3 chipotle chiles (from a can of chipotle
chiles in adobo sauce)
2 teaspoons ancho chile powder
1 teaspoon ground cumin
6 garlic cloves
¼ cup pale ale
1 teaspoon kosher salt
Juice of ½ lime

Pour all the ingredients into a food processor and blend until liquid. Taste with a chip and adjust seasoning.

## fresh pineapple–jalapeño salsa

*For about 2 cups salsa*

1½ cups finely chopped fresh pineapple
1 jalapeño chile, finely chopped (remove
seeds to reduce heat)
¼ cup finely chopped red onion
Juice of ½ lime
¼ cup finely chopped fresh cilantro

Combine all the ingredients and serve!

# HOW TO CHEESE BOARD

A ⬤YUM RECIPE

Cheese boards are one of my favorite things. In addition to tasting delicious, they are the ultimate in party host cheats. All they require is some fridge space and a curatorial eye, and you'll have a platter that any guest would be happy to snack on. Some nights if I have a few girlfriends over, I'll just throw together odds and ends from the fridge with some cheese and we'll make an evening of it.

Be sure to ask a lot of questions and taste everything when you're buying at the local cheese shop. Once you know what cheeses you like, you can start building a board. Every board should have some of these components:

- **Cheese.** I usually do 3 to 5 cheeses in different textures and flavors. Plan on 3 to 4 ounces of cheese per person. Make sure to label each cheese. Guests can then decide which cheese they'd like to try and even jot down the name if they want to buy it for themselves. Keep stronger cheeses on their own plate, or not too near the mild cheeses, so they don't turn off less adventurous guests. Pull the cheese out of the refrigerator 30 to 45 minutes before serving, depending on the temperature outside. You want the cheese to be just below room temperature. If it starts to look slick or greasy, it has been out too long.

- **Fresh fruit.** Apples, pears, figs, grapes, and persimmons are fantastic with cheese. Anything with a honeyed flavor is usually a safe bet.

- **Something briny.** Cornichons, pickled vegetables, whole-grain mustard, and olives are a great counterpoint to rich cheese.

- **Preserves.** If your favorite fruit is out of season, preserves are also delicious, especially spread on some bread. Membrillo (quince paste), fig jam, and apple jelly are good starting points.

- **Meat.** Cured meat and cheese are natural partners. Try to buy your meat and cheese together, so you can choose meat that won't overpower the cheese. Prosciutto's delicate flavor goes with almost anything, and bresaola's mustiness is perfect with an earthy goat or sheep's milk cheese. Spicy salami like chorizo or soppresata is full of flavor, so serve with cheeses that complement them.

- **Bread.** Serve the cheese board with some kind of bread or cracker. Especially if you're serving gooey or soft cheese—you'll need something to spread it on.

- **Nuts.** Toasted nuts add a delicious texture and warmth to a cheese board. Try a soft cheese with walnuts and honey next time you're snacking on a cheese board and you won't regret it.

- **Knives.** Have a knife for each cheese. You don't necessarily have to have special cheese knives, but make sure to put the right kind of knife next to each cheese. For instance, a hard cheese will need a sharp knife, but a soft cheese can be cut with a butter knife.

To make your cheese board assembly a little easier, I put together some of my favorite combinations: by country, by milk, and a basic board filled with crowd-pleasers.

## SPAIN

This could just as easily be France, Italy, or America, but Spain is a wonderful starting point for a cheese board. Using Spanish cheese and garnishes, this board is a great example of "what grows together, goes together." Serve with Spanish wine like a peppery and juicy garnacha or a white blend from Navarre.

- Spanish cheese (Manchego is a crowd-pleaser.)
- Spanish olives (Manzanilla are my favorite.)
- Spanish Marcona almonds
- Membrillo (Spanish quince paste)
- Thinly sliced ibérico ham or prosciutto
- Sliced sourdough bread
- Black Mission figs, halved

## GOAT

Goat products are becoming more easily available than ever, and highlighting the full spectrum of cheese is a great way to appreciate the subtleties of goat milk. Slightly herbaceous, sometimes chalky, goat cheese is known for having a bright, fresh flavor profile. Paired with fennel-dotted finocchiona and briny whole-grain mustard, the flavors that make goat cheese popular really come out.

- 3 or 4 different goat cheeses (Goat Gouda, fresh chèvre, and a bloomy rind version are a great start.)

- Finocchiona (Italian fennel salami)
- Dates (Medjool are my favorite.)
- Toasted walnuts
- Whole-grain mustard

## BASIC

A luscious triple crème like Brillat Savarin will go quickly, and Gruyère and aged cheddars are total crowd-pleasers. They're all great partners with spicy sopressata, and the homemade chipotle pear spread on a little bread with the cheddar is fantastic.

- Brilliat Savarin or any triple crème
- Gruyère or a French Comté
- Hook's Ten Year Cheddar or any aged cheddar
- Sopressata (spicy Italian salami)
- Roasted grapes (recipe follows)
- Cornichons (small French pickles)
- Pear wedges or apple slices

### roasted grapes

1 bunch red seedless grapes
2 tablespoons extra virgin olive oil
1 teaspoon kosher salt

Preheat the oven to 425°F. Place the grapes on a baking pan and drizzle with the olive oil and kosher salt. Roast for 15 to 20 minutes, until the grapes are wrinkled and slightly caramelized. These taste sooooo good.

## HOMEMADE DATE AND ALMOND LOAF

A  RECIPE

This isn't your typical fruit cake. The splendor of its simplicity rests wholly on the quality of the ingredients used. The trick to this cake is ripe and succulent dates. It creates a rich, sticky, and tender yet solid cake that slices beautifully and is the perfect companion with butter for breakfast or with some honey and Brie on a cheese platter. It is best after a few days sitting in plastic wrap, and can last for weeks in the fridge.

*For one 9 by 5-inch loaf*

¾ cup all-purpose flour
¼ teaspoon baking soda
¼ teaspoon baking powder
½ teaspoon kosher salt
¾ cup light brown sugar, packed
3 cups halved walnuts, toasted
2 cups dates, pitted and halved (Medjool are my favorite.)
1 cup dried Mediterranean apricots (or whatever's sweetest), halved
3 large eggs, at room temperature
1½ teaspoons pure vanilla extract

1. Preheat the oven to 300°F. Grease a 9 by 5-inch loaf pan and line the bottom with parchment paper. Grease the parchment paper, too.

2. In a large bowl, whisk together the flour, baking soda, baking powder, and salt. Stir in the brown sugar, walnuts, dates, and apricots. (I find it easiest to mix with a large spoon, digging from the bottom of the bowl, to coat everything.)

3. In a separate bowl, whisk the eggs and vanilla until pale and frothy, about 5 minutes. Add to the flour mixture and combine until all the fruit and nut pieces are coated with the batter. Pockets of dry ingredients pop up, so combine thoroughly. Spread into the prepared pan, smoothing the top.

4. Bake for 80 to 90 minutes in the center of the oven, until the cake is golden brown and a toothpick inserted into the center comes out clean.

5. Remove from the oven and place on a wire rack to cool.

6. When cool, lift the loaf from the pan. To store, cover tightly with plastic wrap. Wait for a day or two to eat, to let the flavors meld. Cut into small slices with a sharp knife.

## BALSAMIC ROASTED FIGS
## WITH BLUE CHEESE

A  YUM RECIPE

At their peak, figs are earthy and mildly sweet, and delicious to eat alone or with a little honey. But to bring out that sweetness and up the juiciness, I like to bake mine with balsamic vinegar. These can be eaten as a dessert with some whipped cream, or as I have them—as part of a cheese course. Either way, they're fabulous.

*For 3 or 4 servings*

1 pint figs, halved lengthwise
2 tablespoons balsamic vinegar, plus more
    for garnish
2 tablespoons extra virgin olive oil
Kosher salt and freshly ground black pepper
10 ounces blue cheese

**1.** Preheat the oven to 425°F.

**2.** On a baking sheet, drizzle the figs with the balsamic vinegar and olive oil, and sprinkle with salt and pepper. Roast for 15 minutes or until juicy and plumped.

**3.** Plate with the blue cheese and drizzle with balsamic vinegar.

## SEASONAL MOZZARELLA PLATTER

A (YUM) RECIPE

Milky fresh mozzarella is delicious on its own but also has some superlative offshoots, namely burrata. Mozzarella curd delicately wrapped around a combination of sweet mascarpone and cream is just begging to be eaten. The name itself comes from *burro*, meaning butter, because it's so creamy and decadent. At home we almost always enjoy mozzarella with heirloom tomatoes, olive oil, basil, and balsamic vinegar—a classic combination—but here I've created a group of recipes to enjoy mozzarella and all of its iterations year-round.

## burrata with roasted fennel and fresh herbs

*For 3 or 4 servings*

½ fennel bulb
Extra virgin olive oil, for drizzling
Kosher salt and freshly ground black pepper
2 teaspoons finely chopped fresh flat-leaf parsley
2 teaspoons finely chopped fresh basil
One 8-ounce ball burrata, sliced

**1.** Preheat the oven to 425°F. Line a baking sheet with a silicone mat or parchment paper.

**2.** Thinly slice the fennel, spread out on the baking sheet, and drizzle with olive oil, salt, and pepper. Roast for 20 minutes, until golden brown and crisp at the edges.

**3.** Mix the roasted fennel with the parsley and basil and serve over the sliced burrata.

## fresh mozzarella with summer plums and walnuts

*For 3 or 4 servings*

One 8-ounce ball fresh mozzarella
2 or 3 ripe plums (Santa Rosa, if you can find them)
½ cup walnut halves, toasted
2 tablespoons balsamic vinegar

Slice the mozzarella and plums. Sprinkle with the walnuts. Drizzle with a little balsamic vinegar.

## burrata with fig "carpaccio" and speck

*For 3 or 4 servings*

3 ripe figs
1 ounce arugula
Extra virgin olive oil
Balsamic vinegar, for garnish
One 8-ounce ball burrata, sliced
¼ pound speck or prosciutto, thinly sliced
1 ounce thinly shaved Parmigiano

Thinly slice the figs. (A mandoline makes this easier.) Dress the figs and arugula with a drizzle of olive oil and balsamic vinegar, and set next to the burrata and speck on plates. Sprinkle with shaved Parmigiano and finish with more balsamic vinegar.

## stracciatella and radicchio

*For 3 or 4 servings*

3 tablespoons unsalted butter
1 garlic clove, minced
1 head radicchio, sliced ½-inch thick
Kosher salt and freshly ground black pepper
⅓ cup white wine
2 tablespoons toasted pine nuts
One 8-ounce ball burrata
Balsamic vinegar, for garnish
Extra virgin olive oil, for garnish

1. Melt the butter in a large sauté pan over medium heat. Add the garlic and cook for a minute until just golden brown. Add the radicchio, season with a little salt and pepper, and cook until wilted and slightly browned. Add the white wine and cook until almost all the liquid is gone.

2. Plate and sprinkle with the pine nuts. Slice open the burrata, remove the insides, and put that on the plate. (That's the stracciatella.) Discard the exterior, or save it in the fridge for later use. (It's just mozzarella, so you can use it as you would fresh mozzarella.) Garnish with balsamic vinegar and olive oil.

## CROSTINI ALL YEAR

A ⬤YUM RECIPE

As I've mentioned, when I go to the farmers' market, I usually black out and don't come out of my food fog until I'm missing $30 and have 6 pounds of fruit and veggies that aren't on my list weighing me down. Cue the crostini.

   None of these takes more than 20 minutes of active time to put together and you can be creative. The topping ingredients listed are per crostini.

### crostini

*For about 50 crostini*

1 baguette (at least 13 inches long), cut into ¼-inch slices, about 50 slices per baguette
½ cup extra virgin olive oil

**1.** Preheat the oven to 350°F.

**2.** Drizzle the bread with the olive oil and put on a baking sheet. (A whole loaf might take up 2 to 3 sheets.)

**3.** Bake for 15 to 20 minutes on the center rack, flip, and bake for another 5 minutes, or until the bread is crisp and toasted.

### roasted garlic and blistered tomato crostini

2 garlic cloves
Extra virgin olive oil, for drizzling
Kosher salt
5 cherry tomatoes
¼ teaspoon finely chopped fresh oregano
Freshly ground black pepper

**1.** Preheat the oven to 425°F.

**2.** Peel the garlic cloves and place on a sheet of aluminum foil. Drizzle with olive oil and sprinkle with salt. Wrap up the cloves and place the package on a rimmed baking sheet in case any oil runs off.

**3.** Place the tomatoes on a rimmed baking sheet covered with a silicone mat or parchment paper. Drizzle with olive oil and sprinkle with salt and pepper. Place both pans in the oven. Roast the tomatoes for 20 to 25 minutes, until blistered and caramelized. Continue cooking the garlic for 25 to 30 more minutes, until the garlic is a deep golden brown.

**4.** Spread the roasted garlic across the crostini, top with the tomatoes and oregano, and drizzle with olive oil.

## ricotta, thyme, honey, and fresh pear crostini

2 tablespoons ricotta
⅛ Bosc pear
¼ teaspoon finely chopped fresh thyme
1 teaspoon honey
Extra virgin olive oil, for garnish

Spread the ricotta on the crostini. Top with the slice of pear and sprinkle with the thyme. Drizzle with the honey and olive oil.

## smashed pea pesto with shrimp crostini

2 tablespoons Pea Pesto (Pea Pesto and Ricotta, page 72)
Extra virgin olive oil
2 small shrimp, peeled and deveined
Kosher salt and freshly ground black pepper

1. Spread the crostini with pea pesto.

2. In a sauté pan over medium heat, drizzle a little bit of olive oil and add the shrimp. Season with salt and pepper as they cook. Cook just until the shrimp are pink and opaque on both sides, about 1 minute a side.

3. Top the crostini with the shrimp and drizzle with olive oil.

## sautéed spinach parmigiano crostini

Extra virgin olive oil
1 ounce spinach
½ garlic clove
Small pinch of chili flakes
Kosher salt and freshly ground black pepper
1 slice Parmigiano

1. Heat a sauté pan over medium heat. Add 1 tablespoon olive oil and the spinach. After cooking for a minute or two (the spinach should start wilting), add the garlic and a pinch of chili flakes, and season with salt and pepper. Continue cooking until fully wilted, about 5 minutes.

2. Put the cooked spinach on top of the crostini and finish with a slice of Parmigiano. Garnish with olive oil.

## goat cheese, arugula, and nectarine crostini

2 tablespoons fresh goat cheese
½ slice speck or prosciutto (if you can't find speck)
2 slices nectarine
A few leaves of arugula
Extra virgin olive oil, for garnish
Balsamic vinegar, for garnish

Spread the goat cheese onto the crostini and top with half a slice of speck. Top with the nectarine slices and a little arugula. Drizzle with olive oil and balsamic vinegar.

# GRILLED CHEESE NIGHT

A **YUM** RECIPE

Sweet, salty, gooey, crunchy deliciousness.
I love grilled cheese sandwiches, and in my
adult years, I've learned how to update this old
classic. Artisanal cheese paired with a touch
of sweet is a mainstay for a cheese board, so
why not take those flavors and sandwich them
between two slices of bread? These are some of
my favorite combinations.

## honey-truffle grilled cheese

*For 2 sandwiches*

4 slices brioche bread
4 ounces Comté or Gruyère, or any mild
  melty cheese, thinly sliced
1 tablespoon honey
Large pinch of truffle salt
2 tablespoons unsalted butter, softened

**1.** For each sandwich, line each piece of bread
with a few slices of cheese. Drizzle with honey
and sprinkle with truffle salt. Sandwich the
slices together and spread the butter on the
outside of the sandwiches.

**2.** Place in a skillet or sauté pan over medium-
low heat and cook until the cheese has started
to melt, about 4 minutes. Flip and cook until the
cheese is completely melted.

**3.** Cut in half and serve.

## date and blue cheese

*For 2 sandwiches*

4 slices sourdough bread
4 ounces sliced or crumbled creamy blue
  cheese (Point Reyes blue or Gorgonzola
  would work well.)
2 dates, pitted and roughly chopped
  (Medjool are my favorite.)
2 tablespoons unsalted butter, softened

**1.** For each sandwich, line each piece of bread with a few slices of cheese. Sprinkle with dates. Sandwich the slices together and spread the butter on the outside of the sandwiches.

**2.** Place in a skillet or sauté pan over medium-low heat and cook until the cheese has started to melt, about 4 minutes. Flip and cook until the cheese is completely melted.

**3.** Cut in half and serve.

## apple jelly, cinnamon, and cheddar

*For 2 sandwiches*

1 tablespoon apple jelly
4 slices white bread
4 ounces sliced English Cheddar
2 tablespoons unsalted butter, softened

**1.** Spread jelly on each slice of bread and stick about 1 ounce of cheese to each slice. Sandwich the slices together and spread the butter on the outside of the sandwiches.

**2.** Place in a skillet or sauté pan over medium-low heat and cook until the cheese has started to melt, about 4 minutes. Flip and cook until the cheese is completely melted.

**3.** Cut in half and serve.

## brie with fig jam and black pepper

*For 2 sandwiches*

2 tablespoons fig jam
4 slices sourdough bread
4 ounces Brie, thinly sliced
Large pinch of freshly ground black pepper
2 tablespoons unsalted butter, softened

**1.** Spread jam on each slice of bread and stick about 1 ounce of cheese to each slice. Sprinkle with pepper. Sandwich the slices together and spread the butter on the outside of the sandwiches.

**2.** Place in a skillet or sauté pan over medium-low heat and cook until the cheese has started to melt, about 4 minutes. Flip and cook until the cheese is completely melted.

**3.** Cut in half and serve.

## fancy ham and cheese with swiss, prosciutto, and caramelized onions

*For 2 sandwiches*

4 ounces Swiss cheese, thinly sliced
4 slices sourdough bread
2 slices prosciutto, thinly sliced
¼ cup Caramelized Onions (page 38)
Freshly ground black pepper
2 tablespoons unsalted butter, softened

**1.** Place a few slices of cheese on each slice of bread. Add prosciutto on one slice for each sandwich and onions on the other. Sprinkle with pepper. Sandwich the slices together and spread the butter on the outside of the sandwiches.

**2.** Place in a skillet or sauté pan over medium-low heat and cook until the cheese has started to melt, about 4 minutes. Flip and cook until the cheese is completely melted.

**3.** Cut in half and serve.

# DRINK RECIPES

## BOURBON MILK SHAKES (GIRLS' MOVIE NIGHT)

A **YUM** RECIPE

When I was growing up, my dad was famous for his milk shakes. To make each one extra delicious, he added half a banana for thickness and texture and a whole raw egg to emulsify and enrich it. If a raw egg isn't your speed, no worries, just don't include it. Here my childhood favorite gets an adult spin with a bit of bourbon.

*For 1 shake, enough whipped cream for 5 or 6 shakes*

**SHAKE**
2 scoops Brown Betty Ice Cream (page 210) or vanilla ice cream
1 ounce (2 tablespoons) bourbon
⅓ cup milk
Pinch of ground cinnamon
1 tablespoon maple syrup
1 large egg (optional)

**WHIPPED CREAM**
½ cup heavy cream
2 teaspoons powdered sugar
1 teaspoon pure vanilla extract

**1.** Blend everything for the shake together in a blender.

**2.** Whip the cream, sugar, and vanilla until soft peaks form. Dollop on top of the shakes.

# BLACK ROSEMARY FIZZ (LADIES' BRUNCH)

AN  RECIPE

Macerated blueberries and blackberries with a touch of rosemary simple syrup make this fizz the perfect combination with gin. For a lighter take, omit the gin and simply add more sparkling wine.

*For 8 to 12 drinks*

**ROSEMARY-INFUSED SIMPLE SYRUP**
1 cup sugar
2 large sprigs fresh rosemary

1 pint blueberries
1 pint blackberries
2 cups fresh lemon juice
8 to 12 ounces gin
8 to 16 ounces sparkling wine or club soda
Ice
Rosemary sprigs, for garnish

1. For the simple syrup, combine the sugar, 1 cup water, and the rosemary in a saucepan. Bring to a boil, then remove from the heat. Allow to steep for about 10 minutes. Strain into a bowl.

2. Combine the blueberries and blackberries in the bowl. Add the lemon juice and syrup. With a wooden spoon, smash a few berries. Allow it to sit for at least an hour in the fridge to macerate.

3. Add 8 ounces of the gin, 8 ounces of the wine, and a cup or two of ice to the bowl.

4. Taste and adjust. Some of us boozy folk prefer less sparkling wine, others . . . not so much, so just mix it to your liking. Ladle into glasses garnished with a sprig of rosemary.

## BLOODY MARY BAR
## (BOYS' BRUNCH)

AN (MMM) RECIPE

I love anything that makes less work for me and more choices for my guests, like a Bloody Mary bar. Set up all of your favorite ingredients and garnishes and let your guests create their versions of the ultimate hangover cure. I love making mine with fresh cherry tomatoes instead of tomato juice and with a touch of sriracha for heat. The results are super refreshing, and much lighter than your typical tomato juice affair.

*For the bar*

Vodka
Tequila
Tomato juice
Worcestershire sauce
Tabasco sauce
Horseradish
Celery stalks
Olives
Kosher salt
Freshly ground black pepper
Cayenne pepper
Lemon juice
Celery salt
Cherry tomatoes
Sriracha sauce
Fresh cilantro
Fish sauce
Ground cumin
Club soda

Set up whichever of the above items you like on a table with an ice bucket, cocktail shaker, glasses, bar spoons, jiggers for measuring, and straws. Let the guests mix Bloody Marys just how they like them.

## fresh bloody mary

*For one 4-ounce drink*

⅓ cup halved cherry tomatoes
1 tablespoon fresh cilantro leaves
Pinch of kosher salt
Pinch of ground cumin
Pinch of celery seeds
1 ounce vodka
½ teaspoon sriracha sauce
½ teaspoon Worcestershire sauce
2 tablespoons fresh lime juice
1 tablespoon pickle or olive brine
Ice
1 ounce club soda (optional)
1 celery stalk

In a cocktail shaker, muddle the cherry tomatoes, cilantro, salt, cumin, and celery seeds. Add the vodka, sriracha, Worcestershire, lime juice, pickle juice, and ice and shake for 15 seconds. Strain into a glass, top with club soda if you wish, and serve with a celery stalk.

## CLASSIC OLD-FASHIONED
## (DATE NIGHT)

A  RECIPE

When you're having someone special over for
a nightcap, the last thing you want to worry
about is a complicated cocktail, so it's best to
stick to the classics. I love good whiskey, and
a decently made Old-Fashioned is a great way
to highlight bourbon's natural sweetness and
spice. My recipe is a pared-down version—no
simple syrup or maraschino cherries—so even
the biggest whiskey snob can enjoy a sip.

*For 1 drink*

1 brown sugar cube (Turbinado sugar has a
    lovely rich flavor if you can find it.)
2 dashes Angostura bitters
2 ice cubes
2 ounces bourbon
1 strip orange peel, removed with a
    vegetable peeler

In a tumbler, sprinkle the sugar cube with the
bitters and crush with a muddler. Add the ice
and bourbon, stirring for 15 seconds to combine. Twist the orange peel over the drink, rub it
on the lip of the glass, and drop in for garnish.

## TOASTED COCONUT VANILLA LIMEADE (BEACH PICNIC)

AN  RECIPE

The toasted coconut in this drink creates a rich, deep flavor that's just dynamite with agave nectar. Add vanilla and lime, and this is the perfect summer drink.

*For 4 to 5 cups, makes 5 or 6 drinks*

1 cup sweetened coconut flakes, packed
10 limes
½ vanilla bean, scraped, or 1 teaspoon pure
    vanilla extract
2½ cups hot water
1½ cups coconut water or regular water if
    you prefer
¼ cup agave nectar

1. Preheat the oven to 350°F.

2. Lightly toast the coconut on a baking sheet, thinly spread out, for 5 to 7 minutes, stirring once halfway through.

3. Juice the limes. Put all the used halves into a bowl, along with the coconut and vanilla bean (or vanilla extract).

4. Cover the lime rinds and coconut with the hot water. Let it sit for about 10 minutes. (The hot water pulls all the natural oils out of the lime skins and adds so much flavor.)

5. Strain the lime-coconut infusion into a blender. Add the coconut water, lime juice, and agave nectar. Blend until just incorporated. Pour into a pitcher and chill in the fridge until ready to serve. Serve over ice.

# BEER FASHIONED (BEER TASTING)

A (YUM) RECIPE

One part Old-Fashioned, the other part beer, inspired by some of my favorite Champagne cocktails, the Beer Fashioned is a summer version of a classic cocktail.

*For 1 drink*

1 brown sugar cube (Turbinado sugar has a lovely rich flavor if you can find it.)
2 dashes Angostura bitters or any other citrus bitters
1 ounce bourbon
1 ice cube
1 strip orange peel, removed with a vegetable peeler
2 to 3 ounces malty beer (An amber ale or Belgian ale is a good choice.)

**1.** Pop the sugar cube into a tumbler and sprinkle the bitters on top. With a muddler, crush the sugar cube. Top off with the bourbon and ice cube. Stir until the ice starts to melt.

**2.** Twist the orange peel over the drink and rub the peel on the rim of the glass. Top off the drink with beer and pop the orange peel into the drink for garnish.

## WHITNEY'S ROSE WATER MINT JULEP (DERBY DAY)

A YUM RECIPE

Whitney is one of my dearest girlfriends, a fabulous sommelier, and a native Kentuckian. Inspired by the rose garlands draped on the winning horses at Churchill Downs, her classic mint julep scented with just a touch of rose syrup is the perfect companion to a derby party. Big hat and seersucker not included.

*For 1 big drink*

4 fresh mint leaves, plus 1 sprig for garnish
1 tablespoon Rose-Infused Simple Syrup
    page 266) or 1 tablespoon simple syrup
    with a few drops of rose water
3 ounces bourbon
Crushed ice
Rose water
2 ounces soda water, plus more if needed

**1.** Tear the mint leaves and muddle in the bottom of a julep cup with the syrup and a few drops of the bourbon.

**2.** Add ice and pour in the bourbon, followed by the soda and a few drops of rose water, if not using rose syrup. Stir with a bar spoon and top off with a little more soda, if needed.

**3.** Garnish with a sprig of mint.

## SANGRIA BLANCA
## (SUMMER DINNER PARTY)

AN  RECIPE

The juicy white peaches and nectarines, along with the strawberries and subtle rose syrup, make this drink a celebration of summer, as the success of the whole thing hinges on the ripeness of the ingredients. I used a torrontes (a South American varietal) instead of a pinot grigio or sauvignon blanc because of its tropical and floral notes. Oh, and don't get weirded out if your rose syrup turns a little green from the fresh rose petals; that's just the chlorophyll doing its thing.

*For 3 large pitchers, makes 24 drinks*

2 white peaches
2 white nectarines
4 oranges (I used a combo of tangelos, blood oranges, and juicy valencias.)
1 pint strawberries
½ cup Rose-Infused Simple Syrup (recipe follows)
Four 750ml bottles torrontes or any nonoaked white wine
Ice

**1.** Slice the peaches and nectarines into eighths or tenths, depending on size.

**2.** You can do whole slices of the citrus, but I prefer cutting supremes, so you can eat them after the fact. Slice the skin off the oranges and slice between the white membrane, segmenting the fruit. Halve the strawberries and set aside in a bowl.

**3.** Add the syrup and wine to the fruit, and let the mixture sit in the fridge for a few hours to combine. Add ice, pour, and enjoy.

### rose-infused simple syrup
⅓ cup sugar
Petals from 1 small, very perfumey unsprayed rose, or ¼ teaspoon rose water

Combine the sugar and petals with ⅓ cup water in a small saucepan. Bring to a boil, remove from the heat, and let sit for 10 minutes to steep. Let the syrup cool to room temperature. Strain.

## SPICY ROASTED PINEAPPLE LEMON-LIMEADE WITH TEQUILA (TACO NIGHT)

AN  RECIPE

Sweet with acid and spice always works. I've yet to meet someone who doesn't like that combination. Here, I could've just as easily used mango and lime with Thai chile, or pear, lemon, and ginger, so if you're feeling creative, go for it!

*For 2 quarts, makes 10 drinks*

5 cups chopped fresh pineapple
    (1 pineapple)
1 red jalapeño chile, thinly sliced (remove
    seeds)
4 cups hot water
4 lemons
8 limes
¾ cup agave nectar
2 cups reposado tequila

**1.** Preheat the oven to 450°F.

**2.** On a baking sheet lined with parchment paper, lay down the pineapple and half the jalapeño slices. Roast for 10 minutes. Remove and set aside the jalapeño. Turn the oven to broil and cook the pineapple for 6 to 7 minutes more, until the pineapple is browned at the edges.

**3.** Juice the lemons and limes. Put all the used halves into a bowl and cover with the hot water. Let it sit for about 10 minutes. (The hot water pulls the natural oils out of the citrus skins and adds so much flavor.)

**4.** Pop the roasted pineapple and roasted jalapeño into a blender and puree. Add some of the water if needed to help the blender get going. Strain into a pitcher.

**5.** Strain the citrus-rind water into the pitcher and add the lemon and lime juices. Finish with the agave nectar and tequila. Add the remaining sliced jalapeño to the pitcher to add color and texture. Chill in the fridge until ready to serve. Serve over ice.

## SPICY YELLOW NECTARINE AGUA FRESCA (BACKYARD BBQ)

A  RECIPE

Sweet, tart, and a little spicy, this refreshing agua fresca is perfect dressed up as a cocktail or dressed down as an easy summer drink. Mix up the flavors with white nectarines, peaches, and any type of orange you like.

*For 6 drinks*

8 yellow nectarines, sliced
2 blood oranges, peeled and sliced, plus
    more for garnish
10 fresh mint leaves, plus sprigs for
    garnish
1 serrano chile, split and seeded, plus more
    for garnish
Juice of 1 lime
3 tablespoons agave nectar

**1.** In a blender, combine the nectarines, oranges, mint, and chile. Puree until completely smooth (add water if you need it to blend). Strain into a pitcher, and add the lime juice and agave nectar (or more or less to taste). Chill.

**2.** Serve over ice with sliced serrano and orange and a few sprigs of mint.

# WHAT WINE SHOULD I BUY?

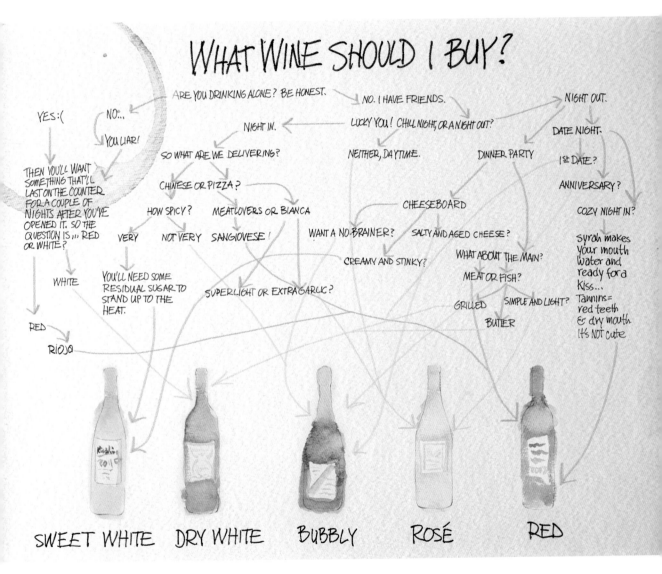

ARE YOU DRINKING ALONE? BE HONEST.

NO. I HAVE FRIENDS.

NIGHT OUT.

YES :(     NO...

LUCKY YOU! CHILL NIGHT, OR A NIGHT OUT?

DATE NIGHT.

YOU LIAR!

NIGHT IN.

1st DATE?

THEN YOU'LL WANT SOMETHING THAT'LL LAST ON THE COUNTER FOR A COUPLE OF NIGHTS AFTER YOU'VE OPENED IT. SO THE QUESTION IS,,, RED OR WHITE?

SO WHAT ARE WE DELIVERING?

NEITHER, DAYTIME.

DINNER PARTY

ANNIVERSARY?

CHINESE OR PIZZA?

CHEESEBOARD

COZY NIGHT IN?

HOW SPICY?     MEATLOVERS OR BIANCA

WANT A NO-BRAINER?     SALTY AND AGED CHEESE?

Syrah makes your mouth water and ready for a kiss...

VERY     NOT VERY     SANGIOVESE!

CREAMY AND STINKY?

WHAT ABOUT THE MAIN?

WHITE     YOU'LL NEED SOME RESIDUAL SUGAR TO STAND UP TO THE HEAT.

SUPERLIGHT OR EXTRA GARLIC?

MEAT OR FISH?

Tannins = red teeth & dry mouth. It's NOT cute

GRILLED     SIMPLE AND LIGHT?

RED

BUTTER

RIOJA

SWEET WHITE     DRY WHITE     BUBBLY     ROSÉ     RED

# ACKNOWLEDGMENTS

## MY FAMILY

I know I'm biased, but I think I have the best family in the world. Thank you for being so supportive, creative, encouraging, and straight talking! Mom and Dad, I honestly don't know where to begin. I wouldn't know how to pick up a knife or a camera, or have the satisfaction of doing something I love, without both of you. Thank you for being inspirations in my life, and for giving me the push I need to get things done and a warm, fuzzy place to retreat to when life gets tough. I love you!

Amanda, thanks for putting up with the strange kitchen smells and constant pile of dirty dishes for a year. Your support, good advice, sick style, and love mean so much to me.

Henry, I'm so excited about your blossoming into an awesome cook! Thanks for letting me publish your pizza and hamburger recipes; I can't imagine the book without them. I love you so much!

Tina, your fingerprints are all over the baking and dessert chapters. Thank you for showing me how to "cook for compliments" and letting me adapt your recipes. They're close to our family's heart and the book wouldn't be complete without those showstopping desserts.

Erica, Rachel, Benji, and Ian, thank you for being the best cuz bugs! You're more like brothers and sisters to me, and all of you dedicating time to help test recipes and encourage me means so much to me.

Pam and Tracy, thank you for all your help testing recipes (and taste testing!). Your support means so much to me.

To Auntie Ree, Sharon, Nana, and my Aussie family: Even though we're thousands of miles away, your influence on these recipes and on me has had such a significant effect on my life. Thank you for all the fun memories around the kitchen (and definitely the fire pit, Auntie Ree!). I love you all so much!

Spookie, you've been such an amazing friend to my family and to me. Your sense of humor, always-engaging conversation, and loving advice have made such a huge impression on me. I love you!

## MY FRIENDS

Craig, my favorite taste tester, you came into my life when I was knee deep in recipe testing and shooting, and basically cookbook crazy. Thank you for your patience and constant encouragement, and for not pushing me to put hot sauce on everything. I love you.

Yayo: Where do I start? "Thanks for everything" seems to cover it, because truly, you've been such an amazing friend and collaborator throughout this entire process. I'm so proud of the work we've created together and can't wait to see what our new adventures will be.

Christie, you will always be my boo. I feel like this whole thing started with our videos in high school, and I'm gobsmacked where our penchant for fake mustaches and Tarantino references have led me. I love you so much; thank you for being my best friend when I needed one.

Whitney, Whitney, Whitney, other than being a beautiful classy lady who knows how to mix a mean cocktail and pick out a killer bottle of wine, you're also an amazing friend. Thank you for collaborating with me and lending your mint julep recipe to the cookbook—the Derby Day party wouldn't have been the same without you.

## MY WORK FAMILY

Kathryn, you're practically my right *and* left hand, legs too, and probably everything else. I can't imagine a workday without hanging out with you on the couch, plowing through work from under a fuzzy blanket. Thank you for your hard work, long hours, and tireless dedication to looking chic in all black and gold. You're (literally) the best!

Callie, you were there at the beginning, *and* I can't imagine a better partner in crime. Your optimism, encouragement, and low-key music choices helped me get through an overwhelming summer of recipe testing in New York. I'm blessed to know you.

Emily, thank you for all the frustrating grocery runs, pots of coffee, snarky comebacks, and hard, hard work. I needed a girl Friday, and you stepped up to the challenge in a big way.

Tamara, how can I say thank you enough? Maybe all caps? THANK YOU. You've pushed me to places I had only dreamed of going and your constant calm, collected, ultrafabulous attitude has taught me so much. Thank you.

Janis, thank you for having my back through this entire process. Your confidence and common sense helped me create the cookbook I've always wanted to make. Thank you.

Emily, Kate, and Megan, I consider myself the luckiest first-time author (!) in the world to have a team like you behind me. Emily, your encouragement and wisdom have impacted the book and me in a big way. Thank you for letting me feel like I could take chances and

create a cookbook from the heart. Kate, thank you for taking my nervous phone calls and e-mails and giving me the peace of mind to keep going. Your management and motivation helped me so much. Megan, thank you for always responding to me with a smile, and making me feel like there are no stupid questions. You've all been so attentive and collaborative; I couldn't imagine a better team to hold my hand through my first time creating a cookbook.

Dylan and Jeni, thank you for your gorgeous photography and for being such great collaborators. I had such a fun time working with both of you and can't wait to see what adventures you guys go on next.

## MY GREEN DOT FAMILY

You truly are my other family. I've known most of you for over ten years, and you've all been there to pick me up and dust me off when I was still figuring out what I was doing with my life. Thank you for eating all the leftovers, reading the blog, and making me feel enveloped in your support. With a team like you behind me, I feel like I can attempt anything. I love you all!

To the Simpatico girls, thank you for your encouragement and support. I love you guys!

The LA food community, farmers' markets, and chefs that I adore, thank you for the amazing memories and delicious food. I love my town and the people in it. Thank you for inspiring me.

# INDEX